Cultural China Series

*Li Li*

# CHINA'S CULTURAL RELICS

## Unearthed History of 10,000 Years

*Translated by Li Zhurun, Li Mingcheng & Pan Yin*

CHINA
INTERCONTINENTAL
PRESS

**图书在版编目（CIP）数据**

中国文物：英文/李力著；李竹润，黎明诚，潘荫译. —2版
—北京：五洲传播出版社，2010.1
ISBN 978-7-5085-1679-0

Ⅰ.①中… Ⅱ.①李… ②李… ③黎… ④潘… Ⅲ.①文物–简
介–中国–英文 Ⅳ.①K87
中国版本图书馆CIP数据核字（2009）第191273号

# CHINA'S CULTURAL RELICS
## Unearthed History of 10,000 Years

Author: Li Li

Translator: Li Zhurun, Li Mingcheng & Pan Yin

Executive Editor: Su Qian

Art Designer: Tang Ni

Publisher: China Intercontinental Press (6 Beixiaomachang, Lianhuachi Donglu, Haidian District, Beijing 100038, China)

Tel: 86-10-58891281

Website: www.cicc.org.cn

Printer: C&C Joint Printing Co., (Beijing) Ltd.

Format: 720×965mm  1/16

Edition: Jan. 2010, 2nd edition, 3rd print run

Price: RMB 96.00 (*yuan*)

# Contents

# Foreword

The Chinese civilization is one of the four most ancient in the world. Relative to the Egyptian, Indian and Tigris-Euphrates civilizations, it is characterized by a consistency and continuity throughout the millenniums. Rooted deep in this unique civilization originating from the Yangtze and Yellow River valleys, a yellow race known as the "Chinese" has, generation after generation, stuck to a unique cultural tradition. This tradition has remained basically unchanged even though political power has changed hands numerous times. Alien ethnic groups invaded the country's heartland numerous times, but in the end all of them became members of a united family called "China."

Cultural relics, immeasurably large in quantity and diverse in variety and artistic style, bespeak the richness and profoundness of the Chinese civilization. These, as a matter of fact, cover all areas of the human race's tangible culture. This book classifies China's cultural relics into two major categories, immovable relics and removable relics. "Immovable relics" refer to those found on the ground and beneath, including ancient ruins, buildings, tombs and grotto temples. "Removable relics" include stone, pottery, jade and bronze artifacts, stone carvings, pottery figurines, Buddhist statues, gold an silver articles, porcelain ware, lacquer works, bamboo and wooden articles, furniture, paintings and calligraphic works, as well as works of classic literature. This book is devoted to removable cultural relics, though from time to time it touches on those of the first category.

Far back in the 11th century, when China was under the reign of the Northern Song Dynasty, scholars, many of whom doubled as officials, were already studying scripts and texts inscribed on ancient bronze vessels and stone tablets. As time went by, an independent academic discipline came into being in the country, which takes all cultural relics as subjects for study. New China boasts numerous archeological wonders thanks to field studies and excavations that have never come to a halt ever since it was born in 1949. This is true especially to the most recent two decades of an unprecedented construction boom in China under the state policy of reform and opening to the outside world, in the course of which numerous cultural treasures have been brought to daylight from beneath the ground.

Readers may count on this book for a brief account of China's cultural relics of eight kinds—pottery, jade, bronze ware, porcelain, sculpture, painting, furniture, and arts and handicrafts articles. We'll concentrate, however, on the most representative, most brilliant works of each kind while briefing you on their origin and development.

Unfortunately, the book is too small to include many other kinds of cultural relics unique to China, for example those related to ancient Chinese mintage, printing and publication of Chinese classics, traditional Chinese paintings and calligraphy. To cite an old Chinese saying, what we have done is just "a single drop of water in an ocean." Despite that, we hope you'll like this book, from which we believe you'll gain some knowledge of the traditional Chinese culture.

# Painted Pottery

Among all cultural relics found in China, what we categorize as "pottery" was the first to come into being. Archeological documentation shows that the earliest pottery ware discovered so far was produced about 10,000 years ago. It is in fact a pottery jar found in the Immortal's Cave in Wannian County, Jiangxi Province, south China. The jar is also the oldest in such conditions as to allow a restoration in its entirety.

# Origin of Pottery Art

For people in the earliest stage of human development, it is earth on which they lived that gave

them the earliest artistic inspiration. That may explains how the earliest pottery was made. The process seems pretty simple: mixing earth with water, shaping the mud by pressing and rubbing with hands and fingers until the roughcast of something useful was produced, placing the roughcast under a tree for air drying and then baking it in fire until it becomes hardened. Before they began producing clay ware, prehistory people had, for many, many millenniums, limited themselves to changing the shapes of things in nature to make them into production tools or personal ornaments. For example, they crushed rocks into sharp pieces for use as tools or weapons, and produced necklaces by stringing animal teeth or oyster shells with holes they had drilled through. Pottery making, however, was

Picture shows a white pottery vessel of the Longshan Culture, which was unearthed at Weifang, Shandong Province.

revolutionary in that it was the very first thing done by the human race to transform one thing into another, representing the beginning of human effort to change Nature according to Man's own design and conception. Prehistory pottery vessels are crude in shape, and the color is inconsistent because their producers were yet to learn how to control the temperature of fire to ensure quality of what they intended to produce. Despite that, prehistory pottery represents a breakthrough in human development. Regretfully, scholars differ on exactly how and when pottery—making began. According to a most popular assumption, however, prehistory people may have been inspired after they found, by accident, that mud-coated baskets placed beside a fire often became pervious to water.

# Development of Painted Pottery

At first, pottery vessels were produced just for practical use, as their producers had no time and energy to spare to "decorate" their products for some sort of aesthetic taste. Among the earliest pottery ware unearthed so far, only a few containers have crude lines painted red round their necks. As life improved along with development of primitive agriculture, people came to have time to spare on undertakings other than for a mere subsistence—crop farming, hunting, animal raising, etc. While still serving people's practical needs, pottery became something denoting people's pursuit of beauty as well. Painted pottery came into being as a result,

Picture shows a pottery jar of the Yangshao Culture that existed 5,600 years ago, which was unearthed at Dadiwan, Qin'an County, Gansu Province. The upper part of the jar takes the shape of a human head.

representing a great leap forward in the development of pottery-making. Among prehistoric relics we have found, painted pottery ware are the earliest artifacts featuring a combination of practical use and artistic beauty. Painted pottery—making had its heyday 7,000–5,000 years ago, during the mid- and late periods of the New Stone Age. The most representative painted pottery ware, mostly containers and eating utensils, were produced in areas on the upper and middle reaches of the Yellow River including what is now Gansu and Shaanxi provinces, on which decorative lines and animal figures painted in color are found.

Without furniture with legs, prehistory people just sat on the ground when they ate or met. For this reason, decorative patterns and figures were painted on parts of a pottery vessel fully exposed to view—for example, the part below the inner or outer side of the mouth of a bowl and, in some cases, decorations on the inner side extending to the bottom. On a basin with an extruding belly, we find decorative patterns below and on the fringe of the mouth and above the curve. In comparison, no decoration is seen below the curve because people sitting on the ground can hardly see that part. In the case of a large basin, decorative patterns are found inside, on the upper side of the inner wall. These are not on the outer wall, because people sitting round the basin cannot see it. Decorative patterns are found on the outer wall of a jar, mostly on the shoulder or above the belly. Small bottles in the shape of a gourd have decorative patterns all over them.

Picture shows a pottery pot produced 4,500–3000 BC, which was unearthed at Qin'an, Gansu Province. It features a slender neck and a painted pattern resembling the face of a pig.

# Painted Pottery of the Yangshao Culture

Painted pottery of the Yangshao Culture is recognized as the most representative of the prehistory painted pottery found in China. Back in 1921, ruins of a primitive village were found at Yangshao Village, Mianchi County, Henan Province, which were to be identified as belonging to a highly developed matriarchal society existed in central China. Many cultural relics have been unearthed from the site since then. Included are pottery utensils for daily use, which are valued not only for their cultural importance but also for the workmanship with which they were produced. Earth to be used for making the roughcasts with was rinsed and, for that, most products are of the same color as their roughcasts. To be more precise, products produced with roughcasts of fine mud are red, and those produced with roughcasts of fine mud mixed with fine grains of sand are brownish red. Most decorative patterns were painted in black, and the rest in red. Sometimes a thin layer of red or white coating was applied to the roughcasts, on which decorative patterns were then painted, in order to ensure a greater contrast of the colors. The Yangshao Culture dates back to

Here is a painted pottery bowl of the Dawenkou Culture that existed 4,500–2,500 BC. It was unearthed at Peixian County, Jiangsu Province.

Painted pottery jars produced 3,000-2,000 BC which belong to the Majiayao Culture.

a period from 5,000 BC to 3,000 BC. Primitive sites and ruins found later in other parts of central China are culturally similar to the Yangshao ruins. For that, the Yangshao Culture has been recognized as synonym of the culture prevalent in central China during the matriarchal clan society—in a region with Gansu, Shaanxi and Henan as center while encompassing Hebei, Inner Mongolia, Shanxi, Qinghai, as well as parts of Hubei. In 1957, the so-called "Miaodigou branch of the Yangshao Culture" became known with excavation of a primitive site at Miaodigou in Sanmenxia City, Henan Province, which archeologists believe existed during the transition of the Yangshao Culture to the Longshan Culture. Painted pottery utensils found at Miaodigou were produced around 3,900 BC. Flying birds, distorted bird patterns done with crude lines and frogs in a style of realism are the main patterns on them.

Fish and distorted fish patterns, sometimes with fishing net patterns, characterize pottery utensils found at Banpo in Shaanxi Province. Archeologists believe these represent another branch of the Yangshao Culture, which is earlier than the Miaodigou branch. Images of frogs are painted on the inner side

**The Longshan Culture**
It is generally referred to the culture of the late Neolithic age in the middle and lower reaches of the Yellow River in China. It was named after the town of Longshan when the cultural relics were found at Chengziya in Longshan town, Zhangqiu county of Shandong province in 1928. At this cultural relics site, wheel-made, highly polished black pottery and thin—walled eggshell pottery utensils were frequently found, therefore, it was also called black pottery culture, and was later renamed the Longshan Culture. The Longshan Culture had its influence in the expansive middle and lower reaches of the Yellow River. The cultural connotations in different regions were different, and the origins of the culture were also different, so it was, as a matter of fact, not a single archaeological culture. In terms of the social development, it belonged to the age of patri-clan social age.

Picture shows a painted pottery cup produced 3,000–2,000 BC. Identified as of the Tanshishan Culture, the cup was unearthed at Minhou, Fujian Province.

Picture shows a painted pottery pot in the shape of a boat, a relic of the Yangshao Culture that existed 4,800–4,300 BC. It was unearthed at Baoji City, Shaanxi Province.

of pottery basins found at Banpo, and deer are the only animal figures on Banpo pottery ware.

What merit even greater attention, however, are painted pottery utensils found at a place also called "Miaodigou" on the foot of Mt. Huashan in Shaanxi. These are beautiful with strings of decorative patterns painstakingly designed and arranged. Research has led to the discovery that the workmen first used dots to mark the position of each pattern on the roughcast of a utensil, and then linked the patterns with straight lines or curved triangles to form a decorative

A painted pottery jar produced 2,000–1,500 BC. It was unearthed at Aohan Banner (county), Inner Mongolia Autonomous Region.

Produced 4,800–4,300 BC, this pottery basin is one of the cultural relics unearthed at the Banpo ruins of the New Stone Age in Xi'an, Shaanxi Province. The decorative pattern features a human face with two fish in the mouth.

belt vigorous and rhythmic in artistic style. A careful viewer won't miss those lines cut in intaglio or relief, forming rose flowers, buds, leaves and stems. Pottery utensils of the same Yangshao Culture that are found in different places invariably have different theme patterns for their decorative belts. Nevertheless, patterns with rose flowers as the theme decoration are found on pottery of all types, indicating an inherent link of theirs.

Discovery of the Banpo Neolithic Village in 1954 is regarded as an important supplement to studies of the Yangshao Culture. Ruins of the primitive village that existed over a period from 4,800 BC to 4,500 BC are in perfect conditions. Decorative patterns on pottery utensils unearthed from there take the shape of human faces, fish and deer and other animals, and archeologists link them to witchcraft characteristic of primitive religions.

One example is a pottery kettle with the ends bent upward and fishing net-like patterns painted on its body—obviously modeled after a primitive dugout canoe which, archeologists say, expresses

Here is a pottery vase of the Yangshao Culture, on which a stork, a fish and a stone ax are painted. The vase was unearthed at Yancun Village, Linrui County, Henan Province.

hope of its producer for a good catch and should have something to do with primitive witchcraft. Mysteries surrounding some human face-like patterns remain to be cracked. Most "faces," so to speak, are round and have straight noses and long, narrow eyes with triangular dunce caps on, as well as fish dangling from both corners of the mouth or on the forehead. Archeologists attribute such patterns to wizards chanting incantations for a good catch of fish.

Patterns of astronomical phenomena should be attributed to primitive agriculture and to understanding of astronomy by prehistory people. Some patterns are realistic in style, with the sun and moon, for example, painted as they actually look like. But in most cases techniques of symbolism were used, with the bird symbolizing the sun and the frog, the moon. Research has led to the conclusion that primitive Chinese thought the bird was the soul of the sun and the frog, the soul of the moon.

Bird and frog images are found on painted pottery produced not later than 7,000 years ago. Those on some of the earliest works are quite realistic in style but, as time went by, such images became increasingly geometrical and mysterious. Use of bird and frog images as theme patterns had continued for well over 3,000 years until the bird image changed into a golden crow and the frog image, into a toad with three legs. In classical Chinese poetry and essays, the sun is often referred to as the "golden crow" and the moon, as the "magic toad."

Bird and fish images in decorative patterns on prehistory pottery can also be seen as totems. Different clans or tribes had different ancestral roots, hence their different totems. Struggles or alliances between different clans or tribes found an artistic expression in patterns picturing fights or unions between different animals. A pottery vase unearthed in Linru County, Henan Province, is a typical case in point. The vase is painted with a picture 37 centimeters tall and 44 centimeters wide, depicting a fierce-looking white stork with a fish, stiff and motionless, in its long beak. A large stone ax is seen at the right side of the bird, with the handle wrapped in pieces of a textile or with a rope wound round it, on which signs that look like alphabet X are painted. The ax might be symbol of the powers enjoyed by the chieftain of a tribe. The bird is done without an outline, its color, pure white, posing a sharp contrast to the fish and ax done with black outlines. It seems that prehistory artists already knew how to increase the artistic effect of their works by using such techniques as contrast.

# Prehistory Pottery Later than Those of the Yangshao Culture

Archeologists have also found whole arrays of primitive pottery utensils as old as those of the Yangshao Culture or produced later. These belong, separately, to the Hongshan Culture of northeast China, Dawenkou Culture of Shandong Province, Majiayao Culture of northwest China and Qijia and Xindian Culture that came later, Daxi and the Qujialing Cultures of southern China, and the Yunshishan Culture prevalent in coastal areas of southeast China. Even places like Xinjiang and Tibet are home to prehistory ruins from where painted pottery utensils have been excavated. A limited number of painted pottery utensils have been found in some prehistory

sites in Taiwan Province, including Dawenkeng at Taibei and Fengbitou at Gaoxiong. These are seen as material evidence to contacts between prehistory Chinese on either side of the Taiwan Strait.

Picture shows a pottery jar identified as of the Majiayao Culture, which was produced 3,300–2,900 BC. It was unearthed at Lintao County, Gansu Province.

# Jade Artifacts

Jade artifacts date back to the middle or late period of China's primitive society about 7,000–5000 years ago, almost as old as painted pottery.

# "Beautiful Stones" and Jade

In making and polishing stone tools, prehistory Chinese found that some stones are exceptionally beautiful with smooth surfaces and lustrous colors. Such stones were broadly referred to as *yu*, which means "jade." In *Studies of the Principles on Composition of Characters*, the very first Chinese dictionary compiled by Xu Shen of the Eastern Han Dynasty (25–220), the character yu is denoted as "beautiful stones." The so-called "beautiful stones" are not exactly what is termed as "jade" in modern mineralogy. Modern mineralogy classifies jade into "hard jade," in fact jadeite, which is as hard as glass or even harder, and "soft jade," which is less hard than glass. To put it in scientific language, hard jade has a 7-degree Vicker's hardness or greater, while soft jade is leas hard. "Beautiful stones" are none other than "soft jade," which is good for carving. Jade, or "soft jade" to be exact, became the sole "beautiful stone" for making art objects with during the Shang-Zhou period (1,600–256 BC). The earliest jade artifacts known to us are personal ornaments produced about 7,000 years ago, including hairpins for men, as well as beads and eardrops. Immediately after their birth, jade artifacts came to be valued for a unique

Picture shows a jade dragon with a pig head unearthed at Jianping, Liaoning Province. It belongs to the Hongshan Culture that existed about 5,000 years ago.

aesthetic beauty relative to stone, wooden, bone and pottery objects and were taken as symbols for monarchical powers represented by military chieftains and divine powers by wizards. In the most recent three decades, large numbers of jade artifacts have been unearthed from tombs of aristocrats that date back to the Neolithic Era, the Shang-Zhou period and the Qin and Han dynasties. Some of these belong to the Hongshan and Liangzhu Cultures.

# Jade Artifacts of the Xinglongwa Culture and Hongshan Culture

Scholars and expert, based on the then archaeological finds, used to believe that the earliest jade carvings in China were from the Hongshan Culture in the north, dating back to 6,700–5,000 years ago. In the 1980s and 1990s, a quantum of jade carvings, more than 1,000 years earlier than the Hongshan Culture, were discovered in the extensive cultural ruins at Xinglongwa in the Aohan Banner, Chifeng city in the Inner Mongolia autonomous region. It was determined that the Xinglongwa cultural ruins dated back to 6,200–5,400 BC, the middle of the Neolithic age, and it was 7,000–8,000 years back from now. Because the mineral property of the Xinglongwa jade wares was the category of actinolite and tremolite, that is, the "*yu*" in the narrow sense mentioned above, or soft jade in terms of mineralogy, the archaeologists affirmed that Xinglongwa jade wares were the

Jade rings unearthed from Xinglongwa in Aohan Banner, Inner Mongolia.

earliest true jade in China, and the world as well.

To date, more than 50 pieces of Xinglongwa jade wares have been found. The jade wares are generally small in size, and their types are mainly the ring-shaped jade ornaments (eardrops) and jade pendants (pieces of jade connected for use as a kind of necklace) in the adornment category and mini jade axes and jade chisels in the category of tools. Most of them were polished without any decorative patterns, showed the most original features of the earliest jade wares, and also born the traces from the Mesolithic age.

Judging from the choice of stone and the making techniques, Xinglongwa jade wares had already reached a fairly high level. First, the people of Xinglongwa had already had a good understanding about the smooth and translucent attributes of jade, and could distinguish real jade from general stone, and it is widely believed that this helped lay a foundation for the development of the Chinese jade culture. Second, they had, apparently, mastered the basic techniques for jade processing as cutting, drilling and polishing, and had known the polishing technique with the pulverizing sand as the medium. All these helped lay a solid foundation for jade wares to become part of the holdings of the art treasure house.

The Hongshan Culture existed about 5,000–6,000 years ago, in areas drained by the Liaohe and Xilamulun rivers in Northeast China. Jade artifacts of the Hongshan Culture are recognized as unique in workmanship and regional character. In terms of the stone property, types and the processing techniques, Hongshan jade wares shared distinctive features with Xinglongwa jade wares, and had a kind of evolution relation.

Most of Hongshan jade wares take the shape of

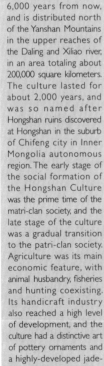

**The Hongshan Culture**
The Hongshan Culture dates back about 5,000–6,000 years from now, and is distributed north of the Yanshan Mountains in the upper reaches of the Daling and Xiliao river, in an area totaling about 200,000 square kilometers. The culture lasted for about 2,000 years, and was so named after Hongshan ruins discovered at Hongshan in the suburb of Chifeng city in Inner Mongolia autonomous region. The early stage of the social formation of the Hongshan Culture was the prime time of the matri-clan society, and the late stage of the culture was a gradual transition to the patri-clan society. Agriculture was its main economic feature, with animal husbandry, fisheries and hunting coexisting. Its handicraft industry also reached a high level of development, and the culture had a distinctive art of pottery ornaments and a highly-developed jade-making trade.

animals, including turtles, fish hawks, cicadas and dragons, and are just three or four centimeters long with holes drilled through—obviously personal ornaments hanging from the belts of their owners. A jade dragon, 26 centimeters long, lays coiled like alphabet C. It is too large and heavy to be used as a personal ornament. Jade dragons similar in shape but much smaller have been identified as belonging to the Hongshan Culture,

Picture shows a coiled jade dragon, an art object of the Hongshan Culture that existed about 5,000 years ago. It was unearthed at Wenniute banner, Inner Mongolia.

inferring that the larger jade dragon could be the symbol of something supernatural that held people in awe. To be more specific, the artifact could be hung for worshipping on some special occasions, say at sacrificial ceremonies. If the inference is correct, we may say that jade artifacts were no longer used purely as ornaments in times of the Hongshan Culture. Time had begun for use of jade artifacts as ceremonial objects as well.

# Jade Artifacts of the Liangzhu Culture

Back in the early 20<sup>th</sup> century, in Shanghai, adventurers and merchants from the West were able to buy some jade artifacts unique in shape and strange in design. One is a long hollow piece of jade carved with images so strange that it was difficult, if not impossible, to tell whether they were human or supernatural. People had no idea of where, when and for what purpose the jade piece was produced, including even the person who sold

**The Liangzhu Culture**
The Liangzhu Culture was one of the Neolithic cultural ruins in China, and was so named after its discovery in Liangzhu town in Yuhang, Zhejiang province in 1936. It was mainly distributed in the Taihu Lake region in the lower reaches of the Yangtze River, and dates back about 5,300–4,000 years. The biggest feature of this cultural ruin was jade ware unearthed. In addition, pottery unearthed there was also very finely-made, and written characters and city were beginning to take shape.

This jade turtle shell is a relic of the Hongshan Culture that existed 5,000 years ago. It was unearthed at Jianping, Liaoning Province.

Here is a jade object that takes the shape of a crown, a relic of the Liangzhu Culture. It was unearthed at Yuyao, Zhejiang Province.

Picture shows a jade ornament of the Liangzhu Culture dating to 2,000–1,500 BC. It was unearthed at Yuyao, Zhejiang Province.

it. Two or three decades later, in Yuhang County of Zhejiang Province, east China, archeologists found some jade artifacts identical in shape and design to the piece mentioned in the proceeding paragraph, but they were still at a loss for when such objects were produced. It was not until the 1980s did experts conclude that these relics belong to the Liangzhu Culture dating back to 3,500–4,000 years ago in some areas on the lower reaches of the Yangtze River. This came after excavations on Mt. Caoxie and Mt. Zhangling in Wuxian County, Jiangsu Province, during which numerous jade artifacts of the Neolithic Age were found, including *cong* (long, hollow pieces with triangular sides), *bi* (round piece with a hole in the middle), as well as *yue* (battle-ax). Likewise, the Shanghai jade piece sold in the early 20th century was identified as a typical art object of the Liangzhu Culture.

Jade artifacts of the Liangzhu Culture are found mainly in Jiangsu, Zhejiang and Anhui provinces on the lower reaches of the Yangtze River. A social estate system was already in place in these areas when these were produced, under which the privileged depended, in addition to forces of arms, on divine power and witchcraft to run roughshod over their subjects, the majority of the local people. That may explain why we attribute most jade artifacts of the Liangzhu Culture—*cong*, *bi* as well as objects that take the shape of hats, semi-circles or three-throng spears—to primitive witchcraft and worshipping of the supernatural. As a matter of fact, these artifacts are often geometrical in shape with symmetrical patterns engraved on them, in a style that denotes solemnity. While the largest in size, *cong* pieces—those long, hollow pieces with triangular sides—outnumber jade artifacts of all other types belonging to the Liangzhu Culture. It is a long time since we began taking note of the decorative designs on jade artifacts of the Liangzhu Culture— particularly on those used at sacrificial ceremonies—that feature animal faces complete with eyes, noses, mouths and other organs. Despite that, discovery in 1986 of the largest *cong*, or the "king of *congs*" as it was dubbed later, still took us by surprise. The "king," which is 8.8 centimeters long and 17.6 centimeters in diameter and weighs 6.5 kilograms, was unearthed from an ancient tomb on Mt. Fanshan, Zhejiang Province. Animal faces in neat groups are engraved on its surface, with the lines recognized as the most elaborate for jade artifacts of the Liangzhu Culture. Each group consists of two parts. The upper part is an inverted trapezoid, which

Picture shows a jade *cong* produced 3,300–2,200 BC, a typical art object of the Liangzhu Culture. For its size, it is dubbed as "king of all *congs*."

bears a broad human face featuring two big eyes, a flat nose, a feather crown and two arms stretching straight and the hands holding the eyes of the image in the lower part. The lower part features a fierce-looking, big-eyed animal face that has a big nose and an oblate mouth. The human head and animal face are cut in relief, and the human arms and animal face, in intaglio. Arrangement of the two parts suggests conquest of a monster by an all-powerful god.

Altogether, 16 such patterns, arranged in symmetrical order, are counted on the "King of all *congs*." It may be worthwhile to mention that this kind of "god vs. monster" design is found on most jade artifacts unearthed from Mt. Fanshan. What merits even more attention is that such a pattern is also found on the upper part of a jade ax-spear, the symbol of military authority. Basing themselves on the symbolic weapon, archeologists have concluded that the design could be the emblem of the Liangzhu tribes and that animal face designs on jade artifacts unearthed earlier could be the simplified or distorted version of the emblem.

# Jade Carvings of the Shang-Zhou Period

Jade carvings of the Shang-Zhou period feature a much better workmanship than Liangzhu jade artifacts. Those excavated from the tomb of a Shang Dynasty royal concubine testify to the truth of this assertion.

The woman, Fu Hao, was a concubine of King Wuding of Shang Dynasty, and her tomb in Anyang, Henan Province, was discovered in 1976 by accident. The tomb is in fact a part of the "Yin Ruins"—ruins of

Here is jade hairpin unearthed at Linxu, Shandong Province, which belongs to the Longshan Culture.

the capital city for the Shang Dynasty in its late period some 3,000 years ago.

Of the 1,600 relics unearthed from the tomb, 755 are jade artifacts, including two dozen exquisitely designed animal and bird figures. Let's see just a few: two hares about to jump, their short tails upward and their long ears against the backs; a tiger with its mouth wide open; an elephant cub with its trunk swaying; and those monkeys that look so cute. The tomb is in fact a zoo of jade animals—real things like elephants, bears, monkeys, rabbits, horses, cattle, sheep, cranes, vultures, parrots, frogs and fish, as well as legendary dragons and phoenixes. There are seven small dragons coiled like alphabet C, inspiring scholars to link them to a large jade dragon of the prehistory Hongshan Culture in their study of the continuity and consistency of the Chinese culture.

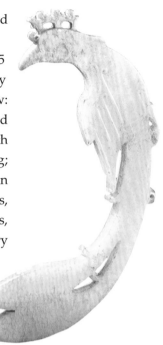

Picture shows a jade phoenix unearthed from the tomb of Fu Hao at Anyang, Henan Province. Fu Hao was a concubine of the last king of the Shang Dynasty.

Two dozen parrots, in fact relieves carved on flat jade pieces, were excavated from the tomb. Two of them share a long tail, their heads arranged in symmetrical order and one side of the tail sharpened like a sword—a perfect combination of artistic value and practical use. By the time of the Zhou Dynasty (1046–256 BC), the status of *bi* had exceeded that of *cong*. In ancient China, what is broadly referred to as *bi*—round flat jade piece with a hole in the center—could be priceless. Here is the story of a priceless *bi*, to which the Chinese proverb "worth several cities," referring to things that are priceless, is attributed.

The story is told in *Historical Records* by Sima Qian (145 BC–?), China's first general history presented in a series of biographies. Back in the Warring States Period (475–221 BC), so the story goes, the State of

Zhao had an invaluable bi in its possession. On hearing this, the King of the Qin State offered 15 cities in exchange for the jade piece. The King of the Zhao had no trust in the king of the Qin, a notoriously treacherous guy, but was afraid that the Qin would invade his land if he rejected the offer. Lin Xiangru, a court official, volunteered to help crack the hard nut and, on his request, he went to the State of Qin with the *bi* as envoy of his king.

As he had expected, Lin Xiangru met with the King of the Qin and offered him the *bi* for a look. When he found that the king of Qin had no intention to honor his promise, Lin cheated him into giving back the *bi* by saying that there was a flaw in the piece and he would show him where it was. With the *bi* in his hands, the man threatened to instantly destroy it before he killed himself by knocking his head on the column against which he was standing. The King of the Qin responded by ordering a map of his state displayed and, pointing at it, he enumerated the 15 cities he would give out in exchange for the *bi*. Lin Xiangru, however, was not to be taken in, and asked the King of the Qin to fast for five days for an elaborate ceremony to celebrate the change of hands for the *bi*. Afraid of losing the *bi* he desperately wanted, the King of the Qin agreed. Immediately after he got to the guesthouse, Lin Xiangru asked a lieutenant to go back with the *bi*. Here is another Chinese proverb originating from the story: "return the jade intact to the State of Zhao," meaning return of something to its owner in perfect conditions.

# Funerary Objects of Jade

According to the *Historical Records*, in 1046 BC the capital city of the Shang was lost to armies of King Wu of the Zhou. Reluctant to be a prisoner of war, King Zhou of the Shang, a most notorious tyrant in Chinese history, set a fire and burned himself to death with a "jade shroud" on. The "shroud," so to speak, consisted of his most valuable jade pieces strung together, which he wanted

Picture shows a blue jade teapot used by Emperor Jia Qing of the Qing Dynasty.

to perish together with him. Far back in prehistory times, it was already believed that jade pieces helped preserve dead bodies. Large quantities of jade artifacts have been excavated from ancient tombs, including even grave clothes made of jade pieces, jade bars in the hands of the dead and jade plugs to gorge the mouth, nose, eyes and ears of the dead with. From tombs of the Liangzhu Culture, archeologists have unearthed jade pieces strung together to cover the dead body with. Nearly 100 jade pieces were found on the cover of the coffin when, in 1990, a tomb of the Gao State of the Spring and Autumn Period was opened for excavation. The

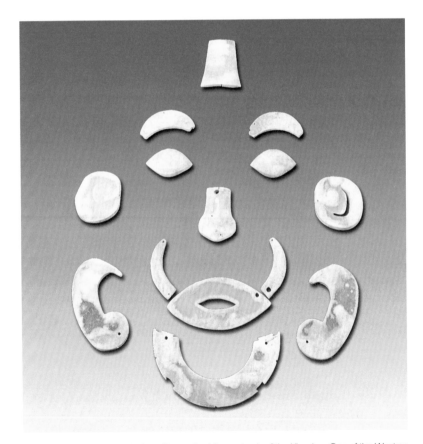

Picture shows parts of the "jade veil" unearthed from a tomb of the Kingdom Gao of the Western Zhou Dynasty (1046–771 BC) at Sanmenxia, Henan Province.

dead body is covered from head to toe with jade pieces. The most remarkable is a piece of textile with small pieces of jade sewn to it, with tiny holes on them to facilitate the sewing. Things like the "jade veil" and the "jade shroud" that perished along with King Zhou of the Shang were to be developed into "jade grave clothes" —in fact sets of small, polished jade chips sewn together with gold, silver, copper and even silk thread. Two dozen such sets have been unearthed from tombs of princes of the Han Dynasty (206 BC–AD 220 ). Each set consists of five "jade cases" separately for the head, the upper part of the body, the lower limbs, the hands and the feet which, put together, assume the shape of a human figure. The jade attire for Prince Liu Sheng of the Western Han Dynasty, which was unearthed from his tomb in Mancheng County of Hebei Province, north China, consists of 2,498 jade chips sewn with 1.1 kilograms of gold thread. The prince's wife shared the tomb with him. She also had jade attire on. Moreover, large quantities of jade ornaments were found in her coffin, the inner walls of the coffin inlaid with as many as 192 jade plates.

# The Bloom of Jade Artifacts

After the Han Dynasty, use of jade artifacts was no longer limited to aristocrats. It expanded to include rich merchants, landlords and scholars keen to display their social status and wealth. This is due to increased communication between China and areas to its west via the Silk Road, which subsequently boosted the country's import of raw jade from Central Asia that encompasses what is now Xinjiang Uygur Autonomous Region. As time went by, jade carvings, in fact carvings of not only "soft jade" but also other precious stones like agate and jadeite, became a thriving industry meeting a huge demand from the upper class. Carving techniques and workmanship improved constantly, especially during the period from the Tang Dynasty to the Song and the period when China was under two successive dynasties, the Ming and Qing.

People seem to forget that once upon a time, in China's slavery society, use of jade artifacts was a part of the social estate system prevalent at the time. As ornaments, however, jade artifacts will remain an important aesthetic choice for the Chinese people.

# Bronze Ware

Bronze is the earliest of all alloys produced by the human race. In China, the earliest bronze ware were produced in the late period of the primitive society, and those produced during the Shang-Zhou period, in large quantities with the production techniques rated as better than ever before, highlight the social estate system practiced at the time. Bronze ware used before the Qin-Han period fall into three categories—those used at sacrificial ceremonies held by the state and aristocratic families, those for daily use by aristocrats and those used as funerary objects. Bronze articles for practical use include weapons, musical instruments, cooking utensils, and food, wine and water containers, as well as ornamental articles on horse chariots.

Bronze weapons unearthed so far are mostly swords, axes, axe-spears and dagger-axes. Bells in complete sets known as *bianzhong* and large bells known as *bo* are the most typical bronze musical instruments played at sacrificial ceremonies and on other important occasions. Tripods and quadripods with hollow legs (*li*), which originated from prehistory cooking utensils, were used to boil whole animal carcasses for sacrificial ceremonies and feasting. Rules based on the social estate system were strictly followed with regard to the use of bronze ware. Nine tripods and eight food containers known as *gui* were allowed on occasions presided over by the "Son of Heaven," the supreme ruler of a state. Aristocrats immediately below the Son of Heaven in rank may use seven tripods and six *guis* or five tripods and four *guis*. In short, the number of bronze containers decreased progressively according to the degrading ranks of the users. There were also stringent rules on the size and weight of the utensils for users of each

A wine vessel of the Shang Dynasty.

A wine vessel and a water container unearthed from a tomb of the Warring States Period in Suixian County, Hubei Province.

rank. Wine sets are in greater variety than any other kind of bronze ware we have found so far—possibly because people of the Shang-Zhou period were fond of drinking wine. The earliest bronze wine sets include *jue* (wine vessel with three legs and a loop handle), *jia* (round-mouthed wine vessel with three legs) and *hu* (square-mouthed wine containers). Many wine containers take the shape of birds or animals.

# Bronze Technology

The earliest bronze artifacts found so far in China—a small knife and fragments of a small knife excavated from Gansu Province, northwest China—were produced during the period from 3,000 BC to 2,300 BC. Bits of copper articles were found from ruins of the Yangshao Culture at Jiangzhai, Lintong City of Shaanxi Province, which are identified as dating back to around 4,700 BC. Archeological findings suggest that the Chinese were producing bronze ware during the period of Longshan Culture that came later, when stone tools were still used.  Bronze, the alloy of copper and tin or lead, has a lower melting point than copper but it is harder. Bronze with a 10% copper content is 4.7 times as hard as copper. Melted bronze alloy expands a little in the course of cooling. For all this, bronze castings have fewer gas holes in them, suggesting that the alloy is good for casting.  Production of bronze ware was a complicated process. Before casting, there was the need to make a die in the shape of the object to be produced. The earliest bronze ware were produced mostly with a single mold and occasionally with two—the upper and the lower—for production of double-faced objects. More than two molds would be needed, including even internal molds, when things more complicated in structure were to be produced. Decorative designs and inscriptions were first carved on the molds, with which casting dies were made. Several dies had to be used to produce a bronze vessel with, indicating that the bronze casting technology was quite sophisticated.

# Bronze Sacrificial Utensils

In the Chinese history, the most famous bronze sacrificial utensils were the legendary "Nine Tripods." In 219 BC, Emperor Shi Huang of the Qin Dynasty sent a task force of more than 1,000 people to salvage nine tripods said to have sunk to the bottom of the Sishui River nearly Pengcheng City in what is now Anhui Province, east China. Legend goes that the nine tripods had been produced on order of the monarch of the Xia Dynasty, the very first political regime set up in the country, as the collective symbol of state power, and were passed down to the succeeding dynasties, the Shang and Zhou. From this legend stems the Chinese proverb "fighting for the nine tripods," meaning "fighting for control of entire China."

According to Zuo's *Commentary*, a historical record

A bronze wine vessel of the Western Zhou Dynasty. It was unearthed from the Yin Ruins at Anyang, Henan Province.

Picture shows a four-legged bronze vessel of the early Shang Dynasty, which was unearthed at Zhengzhou, Henan Province.

covering the period from 722 BC to 406 BC, armies of the Chu State went on a punitive expedition in 606 BC against a rebellious tribe under the jurisdiction of the Eastern Zhou Dynasty that kept the nine tripods. At the border of the Eastern Zhou, the king of the Chu kept asking an envoy from the Eastern Zhou about the weight of the tripods. The story, too, has been passed down from generation to generation. When referring to a careerist bent on seizing the supreme power of the state, people would say the guy "intends to seize the nine tripods."

Altogether, 284 scripts are found on the bottom of this bronze basin of the Western Zhou Dynasty. The basin was unearthed at Fufeng, Shaanxi Province.

Now let's continue with the story about Emperor Shi Huang. After the Eastern Zhou collapsed, the emperor, who was then king of the Qin State, ordered transport of the nine tripods to his capital. Unfortunately, the boat that carried the tripods sank while sailing across the Sishui River. The nine tripods were never salvaged, but the story about Emperor Shi Huang's effort to have them are told in stone and brick carvings in tombs of the Han Dynasty that succeeded the Qin.

Bronze tripods and quadripods were the largest and also the most important sacrificial utensils of the Shang Dynasty (1600 –1046 BC). Many were excavated in the 20th century. Of these, the largest and heaviest, 133 centimeters tall and weighing 875 kilograms, is in the collection of the Chinese History Museum, Beijing. Three characters, reading *Si Mu Wu*, are found on the inner wall of the tripod, "*Mu Wu*" being the title of honor conferred on King Wending's mother posthumously, suggesting that the utensil was produced possibly in honor of the dead woman. The quadripod, square in shape, has two upright ears and its four legs are stout and strong. Animal face and dragon designs are found on the belly of the vessel, and the parts above and below the designs are polished. Each ear features the head of a tiger with a human head in the wide open mouth—a gruesome, mysterious picture, indeed.

Several square-shaped quadripods have been unearthed in recent years in Henan and other provinces. Two of these, though smaller than the quadripod dedicated to *Si Mu Wu*, are identified as much older. The larger quadripod is 100 centimeters tall and 86.4 kilograms in weight. Both belonged to the supreme rulers of the Shang, for use as sacrificial vessels. Relative to the quadripod dedicated to *Si Mu Wu*, they are deep and have short legs.

Bronze utensils other than tripods and quadripods were also indispensable at sacrificial ceremonies and feasting. These include containers for sacrificial animals, food, water and wine, all featuring excellent workmanship and exquisite decorative designs that testify to the importance attached by Shang rulers to those events.

# Decorative Designs and Inscriptions on Bronze Ware

Of those decorative designs found on bronze ware of the Shang, the most eye-catching are those of ferocious-looking animals. A typical design of this kind features a full animal face which, with the bridge of the nose cut straight in the middle, has the eyes, eye brows and horns arranged in symmetrical order at either side. Below the bridge of the nose we find the nose that turns upward and the mouth wide open. In some cases, a claw is found at either side of the head, and the claws are deliberately made small, so small that the face, in the eyes of the viewer, looks even more conspicuous. In some other cases, a body, a leg, a claw and a tail are seen at either side of the animal face. At a first glance, it seems that two bodies have the same head. The true fact, however, is that there is just one animal with its legs and claws set apart because of difficulties for ancient Chinese workmen to present, by casting, a complete picture of the animal's stature.

According to the Collection of Bronze Ware and Stone Carvings with Illustrations compiled during the Northern Song Dynasty, those ferocious-looking images on bonze ware of the Shang Dynasty are the mythical *taotie*, a "voracious man-eater without a body." This assertion is not entirely correct. In the first place, such images do have bodies, and the bodies are quite conspicuous on some of the earliest bronze ware. Secondly, images on bronze ware often have horns that look like cattle or sheep horns, while *taotie* does not. In our opinion, these images were deliberately made ferocious or mythical to arouse a kind of reverend awe for bronze ware owners. This kind of artistic effect was exactly what aristocrats wanted to achieve by having bronze ware made.

Ferocious-looking designs are not the only decorations on bronze ware left over from the Shang Dynasty. We also find on

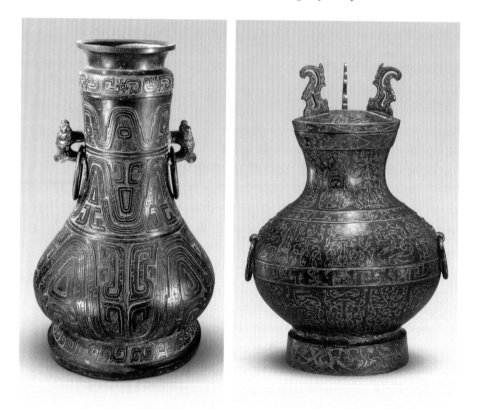

Picture shows a bronze pot of the mid-Western Zhou Dynasty, which was unearthed at Fufeng, Shaanxi Province. The pot bears 60 scripts in 12 lines.

Photo shows a bronze pot unearthed from the tomb of Prince Liu Sheng of the Western Han Dynasty. The pot is inlaid with ancient scripts of gold and silver wires and decorated with a belt of animal figures round it.

them designs of dragons, cicadas, birds, silk worms and turtles.

Bronze utensils of the Shang Dynasty also have inscriptions on them. Inscriptions on the earliest bronze utensils are limited in number, in most cases just a few, denoting the name of the owner or the most senior elder of his family. Much more inscriptions are found on bronze utensils produced during the period spanning the late Shang and early Zhou, whose numbers range from dozens to hundreds—on one of them, nearly 500, virtually the complete text of an article. These inscriptions are in fact invaluable historical records on what happened in what year, mostly on wars and divinations. One best example is a *gui* (a food container) unearthed in 1976 from a site in Lintong, Shaanxi Province, which has 32 scripts in four lines on the bottom. The text tells the exact date when armies under the command of King Wu of Zhou seized the capital of the Shang under King Zhou. For his role in the battle, King Wu gave the owner of the basin, a nobleman named Li, a quantity of bronze, with which Li had the basin made. The date of the event given in the text is exactly the date in classics of Chinese history including the *Book of Documents* and the *Historical Records*.

# Animal-shaped Bronze Vessels and Bronze Human Figures

Some bronze vessels of the Shang Dynasty take the shape of animals that look strange enough to capture the viewer's fancy. A most striking example is a wine vessel excavated from the tomb of Fu Hao,

An owl-shaped wine vessel unearthed from the tomb of Fu Hao at Anyang, Henan Province. Fu Hao was a royal concubine of the Shang Dynasty.

Pictures shows a human head of gilded bronze unearthed at Guanghan, Sichuan Province, which was produced during the Shang Dynasty (1600–1046 BC).

a concubine of King Wuding of the Shang, in Anyang. The vessel takes the shape of an animal with a head that looks like a horse head but with goat horns. The fore feet of the animal are in the shape of hoofs, which are longer than the hind feet in the shape of bird claws. The thighs have a wing on each and, on the back of the animal there is a dragon with horns. In shape, another wine vessel excavated from the same tomb goes beyond the wildest imagination of the viewer. Seen in the front, a tiger greets the viewer's eyes and looking from behind, the viewer sees a vulture-like bird.

Patterns supernatural in artistic style continued into the Western Zhou Dynasty. A bronze wine vessel unearthed from a tomb of that period at Zhang Jiapo of Chang'an in Shaanxi Province takes the shape of an animal carrying a tiger, with a phoenix and two dragons on its back. The animal's head looks like the head of a bull but with the horns of a dragon and its ears standing erect. Moreover, the animal has hoofs and a pair of wings. The body is decorated with exquisite designs of animal faces, dragons, *kui* (single-leg animal that looks like a dragon) and lightning.

There are also human figures on bronze vessels. One bronze *he* (three-legged vessel used to warm cold wine with hot water in it) features a human face with a pair of dragon horns. The most artistically outstanding is a wine pot with a small mouth and a big belly, which is known to archeologists as *you*. It features a human figure embracing a tiger, his bare feet on the hind paws of the tiger, and his head in the tiger's mouth. The man's face bears no expression of pain or horror, suggesting that the man and the tiger are friends. Some archeologists think that the man could be a wizard and the tiger, his assistant. The wine pot could be a magic instrument by means of which the wizard was supposedly able to communicate with the supernatural world. In ancient times, wizards often exercised witchcraft under the influence of alcohol.

Human figures are also found among bronze artifacts produced during the Shang-Zhou period.

Picture shows a bronze figurine of the Shang Dynasty, which was unearthed at Sanxingdui in Guanghan, Sichuan Province. The figurine, 262 centimeters tall, is the tallest of its kind found so far in China.

While digging in spring of 1929, a farmer at Yueliangwan Village of Guanghan County, Sichuan Province, happened to find a pit full of funerary objects made of jade. In the 1950s, archeologists began their work at the site and, as time went by, a 15 square kilometer-area at Sanxingdui in Guanghan, came to be identified as a treasure house of cultural relics produced 4,800–2,000 years ago.

The site, named as Sanxingdui by experts, has stunned the world archeological community for a unique cultural importance. Among the numerous cultural relics excavated from there, there is a bronze human figure 262 centimeters tall. The statue, barefooted and with a pair of bracelets round the ankles, stands on a platform. It "wears" a long robe with cloud patterns. Also unearthed from the Sanxingdui site are several life-sized head sculptures of bronze, as well as animal head sculptures and masks, which are also of bronze. All the faces are thin, with large, extruding eyes, big ears and square lower jaws, while the mouths are tightly shut. Studies of primitive religions have led to the discovery that the prehistory people invariably worshipped idols in the shape of animals which, as time went by, were replaced by half animal, half human figures and, finally, by supernatural beings in human shape. This process reflected changes in position of the human being in nature. Bronze human figures of Sanxingdui, which are semi-realistic, semi-abstract in artistic style, are the earliest of their kind found in China. From these we may acquire some idea of the physiques and facial looks of the people in the area when these cultural relics were produced.

# Bronze Weapons, Helmets and Shields

Here is a quotation from *Zuo's Commentary*: "Sacrificial rites and wars are the most important state affairs," suggesting that for a long time in ancient China, wars were regarded as important as sacrificial ceremonies. That explains why weapons and shields account for a large proportion of the bronze artifacts we have found so far. The figure is 30% for those from Fu Hao's tomb, next only to that for sacrificial vessels, and the proportion is even greater for less important tombs of the Shang-Zhou period.

Though meant to kill, bronze weapons invariably bear decorative designs. On some swords, for example, we find patterns of exquisite lines and gold-inlaid inscriptions. Decorative designs on shields and helmets look more mythical and fearsome than those on spears, swords and other weapons. No. 1004 tomb of the Yin Ruins in Anyang furnishes a most striking example. Bronze helmets unearthed from the tomb take the shape of animal faces, bullheads with long, curved horns, ferocious-looking tiger heads with big ears, and eyes awesomely large. Shields from the tomb feature long-toothed men or animals with livid faces, obviously to terrify the enemy.

Bronze swords and daggers popular among nomadic tribes in north China often have handles in the shape of sheep, tigers, horses, deer and other animals, in an artistic style good enough to influence the making of such weapons in the country's heartland. What merit special mention are bronze weapons belonging to people of the ancient Dian ethnic group in

**The Yin Ruins in Anyang**
The Yin Ruins are located along the banks of the Huanhe River in the northwestern suburb of Anyang, Henan province. In 273 years of construction from Pan Geng, king of the Shang Dynasty who moved the capital to Yin to Di Xin, the last king of the Shang, the capital was developed into a grand city covering about 30 square kilometers. In the 1890s, oracle bones with inscribed characters for fortune-telling were found at the Yin Ruins. Beginning from 1928, archaeologists started continuous and comprehensive archaeological excavations at the Yin Ruins, and found the ruins of palaces, workshops and tombs, and unearthed a quantum of cultural relics as oracle bones, bronze wares and jade wares.

A bronze battle axe unearthed from the tomb of Fu Hao.

China's deep south, which invariably have animal and bird images on them. Round the mouth of the tube for installing the handle of a spear or axe there are neat groups of animal images including deer, bulls, apes, wolves, snakes and pangolins. Round such a tube for the handle of a sickle-shaped weapon we find three human figures with a bull. A bronze spear enables us to see for ourselves the cruelty of the slavery society by featuring two slaves or prisoners of war with their hands tied behind their backs and their heads drooping. Exquisite lines are found on shields used by warriors of the Dian. The lid of a bronze utensil unearthed from a Dian tomb at Shizhaishan, Jining of Yunnan Province, takes the shape of a warrior with an armor suit on.

Use of bronze weapons kept decreasing in step with a constant increase in the use of iron and steel after the Shang-Zhou period. After China became unified under the Qin, the country's first feudal dynasty, all bronze weapons were confiscated on order

Photo shows a bronze lamp used in Changxin Palace of the Western Han Dynasty, which was unearthed from the tomb of Prince Liu Sheng at Mancheng, Hebei Province. The right arm of the "palace lady," which is hollow, diverts the smoke into her body.

Here is a horse-drawn chariot of bronze, a funerary object for Emperor Shi Huang of the Qin Dynasty.

of Emperor Shi Huang, the dynasty's first and, in fact, China's first, and were replaced by weapons of forged steel. As sculptural art objects, however, bronze artifacts have always important. To name just a few of such artifacts produced during and after the Qin Dynasty: a chariot from the tomb of Emperor Shi Huang, a horse from Gansu with a falcon under a hoof, as well as those lions guarding the Forbidden City and Summer Palace in Beijing. While known worldwide for an artistic beauty, these tell people stories that happened in China for a period of well over 2,000 years.

# Porcelain

The earliest porcelain came into being during the Shang Dynasty (1,600–1046 BC) as a development of pottery. Invention of porcelain was a great contribution made by the Chinese people to the world civilization, for which people in the West often equate porcelain to China. Over the past milleniums, Chinese porcelain underwent roughly four phases of development—the phases of primitive blue porcelain, blue porcelain, white porcelain and painted porcelain. Towards the end of the Tang Dynasty and the beginning of the Five Dynasties, porcelain ware, originally for daily use by ordinary Chinese, became popular among members of ruling class as well. That came when officials sent the best porcelain ware available locally to the imperial palace as tributes, and that led to porcelain production on imperial orders. During the Five Dynasties period, King Qian Miao of the State of Wuyue and Emperor Chai Rong of the Late Zhou Dynasty designated some porcelain kilns to specialize in production to meet their own needs, ushering in what was to be known as "imperial" or "official" kilns. Imperial kilns, so to speak, never cared about the cost of production, so long as their products were good enough in design and quality to invoke the imperial pleasure. For this reason, porcelain ware produced there were always better than products produced elsewhere, and those from imperial kilns of the successive Song, Yuan, Ming and Qing dynasties have always been favorites for collectors worldwide.

# Porcelain of the Six Dynasties

Porcelain production calls for use of porcelain clay with an iron content of around two percent, a temperature not

A wine bottle left over from the Northern Dynasties. It takes the shape of a lotus.

lower than 1,200 degrees Centigrade that makes the product waterproof, and application of glaze to the surface of the roughcast in such a way as to make it even and fast. Porcelain products of the Shang-Zhou period unearthed so far basically meet these conditions. We call them "primitive" because in a sense, they are just "glazed pottery."

Primitive porcelain ware, mostly pots and bowls, have a crude surface, bluish ashy or yellow in color. These

A blue porcelain wine vessel of the Western Jin Dynasty. It was unearthed from a tomb built in the year 302.

were used as water containers as they are more waterproof than pottery ware.

Porcelain production techniques had become quite sophisticated by the time when China came to be ruled by the Eastern Han Dynasty. Porcelain products produced during the Eastern Han Dynasty are rated as good, or nearly as good, as contemporary porcelain products in terms of the quality of the roughcasts and glaze and of the temperature in kilns. For this reasons, Chinese scholars regard the Eastern Han Dynasty, or around 200 AD to be more exact, as the time of birth for porcelain in its true sense.

For nearly 400 years after the Eastern Han Dynasty collapsed, China was torn apart except a short period when the country was unified under the Western Jin Dynasty. Southern China, however, was relatively peaceful while wars were fought in succession in northern China. Thanks to a rapid increase in population that resulted from a mass migration of people from the north, areas south of the Yangtze River were able to enjoy an economic boom to the benefit of handcraft production, porcelain production included. Ruins of porcelain kilns identified as of the Six Dynasties have been found across the length and breadth of southern China, in Jiangsu, Zhejiang, Jiangxi, Fujian, Hunan and Sichuan provinces in particular.

The Six Dynasties, so to speak, all had what is now Nanjing as capital and ruled southern China for well over 300 years in succession, from the early third century to the end of the sixth. They were the Wu of the Three Kingdoms period, the Eastern Jin, and the Song, Qi, Liang and Chen that are collectively known as the Southern Dynasties. What is know as "blue porcelain," porcelain with bluish ashy, light blue and greenish blue as the basic hue, constitutes the main stream of porcelain products produced during the period. What merits special mention are the Yue and Wuzhou kilns in Zhejiang Province. Glaze on the surface of blue porcelain produced there is even and fast, indicating proper control of temperature and the extraction of roughcasts inside the kilns.

Most blue porcelain products of the Six Dynasties are for daily use, the rest being funerary objects. In design and decoration,

A blue porcelain sheep.

however, they are much better than those produced in the past. Many are ingeniously constructed, breaking away with those old geometrical patterns. There are, for example, bird-shaped cups, water containers in the shape of frogs, animal-shaped wine vessels, pots in the shape of eagle, teapots with spouts in the shape of chicken head, as well as paperweights in the shape of crouching sheep. While for daily use, these are artworks in every sense. Let us have a look at a bird-shaped cup unearthed from a Western Jin tomb at Baiguan Township, Shangyu City, Zhejiang Province. The semi-circular body of the cup serves as the belly of a bird with a backward-looking head on one side of the upper part of the body and a fan-shaped tail on the opposite side. The bird, with its wings opening and its legs drawn, looks as if flying. While anatomically correct, a blue porcelain sheep unearthed from Mt. Qingling in Nanjing, Jiangsu Province, looks so docile as if it is real.

## Porcelain of the Sui-Tang Period

The period from the Tang Dynasty (618–907) to the Five Dynasties (907–960) was a landmark for development of China's porcelain art. During that period, white porcelain appeared in northern China and porcelain with underglaze paintings—porcelain with decorative patterns painted or cut on the roughcasts—in the south.

White porcelain features pure white roughcasts and glaze obtained by reducing the iron content in them. The earliest white porcelain vessels were produced under the Northern Qi Dynasty (550–577). Bowls, cups and long-necked bottles unearthed from the tomb built in 575 for Governor Fan Cui of Liangzhou, or what is now Anyang, Henan Province, are recognized as the best representatives of white porcelain in the early stage of its development. Both the roughcasts and glaze of these vessels are opal in color, with the glaze of some slightly blue.

White porcelain production techniques continued to improve

during the Sui and Tang dynasties, with the pure white color more stable and the products more ingeniously constructed to the liking of upper class members. Many small, beautiful white bottles, boxes and pots were unearthed from the tomb built in 608 for Li Jingxun, a great granddaughter of Emperor Wen Di of the Sui, who died at nine. Among these, the most remarkable is a pot with a chicken head and a dragon-shaped handle. The pot, 26.4 centimeters tall, is bright with pure white glaze. The chicken head and the dragon-shaped handle are in a style of artistic exaggeration, making the pot exceptionally attractive. No trace of blue or yellow is discerned in the glaze layer, indicating that white porcelain production techniques had become fairly sophisticated.

White porcelain kilns of the Tang Dynasty were mostly in areas north of the Yangtze River, in Henan, Hebei, Shanxi, Shaanxi and Anhui Province, to be exact. In areas south of the Yangtze River, production of blue porcelain continued to develop. The best-known blue porcelain kilns were in Zhejiang Provinces, alias Yue, hence the

A porcelain pillow of the Tang Dynasty.

"Yue Kilns" as historians choose to call them. Products identified as of the Yue Kilns, mostly bluish yellow or bluish green in color, are as bright and smooth as jade articles. They are in huge varieties—bowls, plates, wine and tea things, as well as lamps, pillows, spittoons, cosmetic powder boxes and inkpads. Large numbers of porcelain vessels produced at the time take the shape of flowers—bowls in the shape of lotus leaves or crab apple flowers, plates in the shape of lotus flower and sunflower petals, etc.

During the period of the late Tang and the Five Dynasties, the Yue Kilns were designated to produce for imperial use. Their products are known as "discreet porcelain pieces" because they were strictly forbidden to people outside the imperial families. In a poem entitled *The Discreet Yue Porcelains*, Tang Dynasty poet Lu Guimeng wrote:

Accompanied by late autumn wind and dew, the Yue Kilns start producing With magnificent hue of the mountains are they bringing.

Though fascinated by the poem, people had given different interpretations to the meaning of "magnificent hue of the mountains" until they were able to see some of the real things. That came in 1987, when huge quantities of relics of the Tang Dynasty were unearthed from the Famen Temple at Fufeng, Shaanxi Province, including 16 identified as Yue or "discreet porcelain pieces" according to an inventory of the relics buried alongside them. Two bowls are bluish yellow in color, and the other pieces are either bluish green or bright green, the glaze on them sparkling and crystal-clear. All of them are ingeniously constructed, featuring a simple, lucid style. Several of them are shaped like plants. One is a water bottle with eight raised edges round its body, which looks like a melon. There is also a plate formed with five flower petals.

Porcelain pieces with underglaze paintings dating to the period from the mid-and late-Tang Dynasty to the Five Dynasties, have been unearthed from ancient kilns in Shangsha of Hubei Province. They represent a breakthrough in the development of China's porcelain art. Porcelain artifacts of the Shangsha kilns are mostly brown or brownish green in color, suggesting that gone were those centuries when porcelain artifacts were almost exclusively bluish. Porcelain artifacts with underglaze paintings were produced by having decorative patterns painted or cut on their roughcasts before glaze was applied. The earliest such pieces are decorated with strings of brown dots and those produced later, with brownish green dots that look more beautiful. Porcelain artifacts of the Changsha kilns are unique in artistic style. The most remarkable are pots with straight spouts or spouts that look like white-edged morning glory, round, long bellies or bellies in the shape of melons or bags. There are also tube-like pots, octagonal pots and pots shaped like a column.

Porcelain objects with "twined roughcasts" represent a new school of porcelain art developed during the Tang Dynasty, for which the Dangyangyu Kilns were most famous. "Twined roughcasts" are produced by mixing white and brown porcelain clay in such a way as to form lines or dots alternately white and brown. Most porcelain objects with "twined" roughcasts that have survived to our time are pillows. In most cases, such porcelain pillows have three round flower patterns arranged in a neat triangle, for which they are known as "flower pillows." The production process was very complicated and that explains why, more often than not, a flower pillow only has the surface "twined" while the part beneath the designs are produced just with white porcelain clay. Back in 1978, experts from the Palace Museum in Beijing unearthed a broken piece of a "flower pillow" from ruins of ancient porcelain kilns in Gongxian County, Henan Province. They found that in thickness, the surface of the pillow, the part with flower designs, accounts for only one third of the roughcast.

# Porcelain Kilns of the Song Dynasty

China's porcelain art enjoyed boomed again during the Song Dynasty (960–1279), when porcelain kilns mushroomed across the country. Archeological surveys conducted since the 1950s show that of the 170 counties in ancient China, 130 have ruins of porcelain kilns left over from the Song Dynasty, which account for 75 percent of the total left over from all Chinese dynasties.

Competition was fierce between porcelain producers, culminating in the birth of what historians call the "five most famous sites for porcelain production in the Song Dynasty"—the Ru, Guan, Ge, Jun and Ding. As porcelain artifacts unearthed from ruins of some of the sites are too few, we have to concentrate on six sites whose status in porcelain production has been established through archeological excavations. These are Dingzhou, Zhaozhou, Jun and Cizhou kilns in north China and the Longquan Kilns famous for blue porcelain and Jingdezhen Kilns famous for white porcelain.

The Ding Kilns are found at Cicun Villages and the East and West Yanshan villages in what is now Quyuan County, Hebei Province. In ancient times, Quyang was under the jurisdiction of Dingzhou, hence the Dingzhou Kilns. The Dingzhou Kilns produced mainly white porcelain, plus a limited quantity of black and purplish brown porcelain. The best known unearthed from the sites are porcelain artifacts yellowish white, the color of ivory. These are often called "cosmetic powder porcelain" for their glaze layer as fine and tender as the skin of young girls with a thin layer of cosmetic powder applied on their faces. Products of the Ding Kilns have decorative patterns done by cutting or engraving on the roughcasts, mostly taking the shape of animals

A porcelain jar of the Song Dynasty. It is a product of the Jizhou Kilns.

or flowers. Those meant for use by the imperial family have dragon-phoenix designs.

The Yaozhou Kilns in what is now Yaoxian County, Shaanxi Province, were among the best known private porcelain producers during the Song Dynasty. Blue porcelain artifacts were their main products. Products of the Yaozhou Kilns are famous for those decorative patterns cut in such a way as to look like relieves. Round a pattern there are fine, delicate lines cut in intaglio that look like ripples or stamens. Products produced during the period of the Five Dynasties are glazed in bright blue, light blue, ashy blue, pea green or deep brown, and those during the Northern Song Dynasty, in olive green or light blue.

The Jun Kilns in Yuxian County, Henan Province, were the most remarkable among porcelain producers of the Song Dynasty. Copper oxide was used by the Jun Kilns as the coloring agent, instead of ferric oxide, the traditional coloring agent for production of blue porcelain. Thanks to use of the new coloring agent and through a complicated process of oxidization and outer flaming, porcelain artifacts bright with a variety of colors were produced. The most

A porcelain pot glazed in blue and with a lid in the shape of a lotus leaf, a representative product of the Longquan Kilns of the Song Dynasty.

fascinating are those azure, reddish black or pale blue in color, which glimmer like stars in the dark blue sky at night. There are also those magnificently crimson like the evening glow. The two main colors, blue and crimson, form the most salient feature of Jun Kilns' products, which represent a breakthrough in the development of China's porcelain art.

The Cizhou Kilns were a complete system of private porcelain producers in Henan, Hebei and Shanxi provinces, in fact the largest of its kind in north China. Cizhou porcelain products are unique, featuring a folk pictures on layers of black or brown glaze. Especially worth mentioning are those porcelain pillows with pictures depicting children angling, putting ducks or quails out for feeding, or whipping tops, which are beautiful with simple, smooth lines. Folk maxims, such as "silence is gold" and "don't stay away from home for too long," are often inscribed on Cizhou porcelain pillows. One cautions travelers to be always on guard against possible risks. Here it goes: "dismount the horse before crossing a bridge, don't travel by boat wherever there is a road, find somewhere to stay for the night before sundown, and set out for the journey when cocks crow; ever since ancient times, most victims of murder have died while traveling."

Kilns producing blue porcelain in Zhejiang Province during the Song Dynasty are collectively referred to as the Longquan Kilns. Products of the Longquan Kilns are bright and smooth like jade, representing the peak of China's blue porcelain art.

Known across the world as "China's porcelain capital," Jingdezhen in Jiangxi Province produced bluish white porcelain during the Song Dynasty. Bluish white porcelain of Jingdezhen in southern China had something to do with white porcelain of the Ding Kilns in the north. Large numbers of handicraftsmen in northern China migrated to areas south of the Yangtze River, after the Song Dynasty lost areas north of the river to the Jin and moved its capital from what is now Kaifeng, Henan, to Hangzhou, Zhejiang. Among them, many porcelain workers settled in

Jingdezhen and Jizhou in Jiangxi, where quality porcelain clay, fuel and water were available. Using these, they developed a kind of fine, almost transparent porcelain that constitutes a sharp contrast to ivory white porcelain of the Ding Kilns. Glaze of an exceptionally high quality makes the bluish color of Jingdezhen porcelain look so natural. It eventually ushered in the birth of porcelain with underglaze paintings.

Also worth mentioning are the Ge Kilns, whose products are reputed for cracks beneath the glaze which, produced by using some kind of additives in the glaze, yield a unique artistic effect. The most exquisite are the so-called "cracks of gold wires and iron thread." Cracks on large areas are produced when a glazed porcelain artifact undergoes the process of cooling in a kiln, and the cracks are then filled with fine earth purplish golden in color. Cracks, though much smaller, continue to form on the surface after the porcelain artifact is taken out of the kiln, and such cracks are then filled with fine, golden earth.

Porcelain artifacts of the Song Dynasty are beautifully shaped. One best example is a porcelain pillow in the shape of a little boy who seems to have a rest after playing. A product of the Ding Kilns in the collection of the Palace Museum in Beijing, the "boy," so to speak, looks naughty, his head resting on his hands with the right hand holding a ball with long tassels hanging from it, and his legs slightly drawing up. The boy's sunken waist is where the head is rests on.

Ancient Chinese liked to use porcelain pillows in summer. It is known that during the Song Dynasty, at least four kilns specialized in producing porcelain pillows. Among porcelain pillows identified as products of the Cizhou Kilns, most have inscriptions indicating that the Zhang family was their producer, and textual research has led to the conclusion that the family business had a history of no less than 300 years. Li Qingzhao (1084– about 1155), a female poet of the Southern Song Dynasty, in one of her best-known poems wrote of a "jade pillow" she used. Historians have proved that this

A Porcelain pillow of the Song Dynasty.

"jade pillow" was in fact a bluish white porcelain pillow produced at Jingdezhen.

# Blue and White Porcelain of the Yuan Dynasty

The Chinese porcelain before the Song dynasties basically maintained its development trend featured by its monotonous color of blue or white, but this trend was changed in the Yuan Dynasty when a new type of porcelain was produced, that is, the globally renowned blue and white porcelain.

Blue and white porcelain refers to a special type of porcelain: The painting was applied to the raw, dried porcelain bodies with cobalt-blue pigment, then the crystal glaze was applied, after they were dried, they were fired only once at a temperature as high as 1,350 degrees centigrade, and the patterns and lines under the glaze became blue. The raw materials for blue and white porcelain, that is, natural minerals with elements of cobalt, were mainly from Yunnan, Zhejiang and Jiangxi, and some were also imported from foreign countries.

The firing and production time of white and blue porcelain was originally believed to be in the Yuan Dynasty. In 1985, a big, damaged blue and white bowl was unearthed from Yangzhou, Jiangsu province. On the bowl, peonies and auspicious cloud patterns were painted, and these patterns were identical with that on the bronze mirrors from the Tang Dynasty. Laboratory tests by researchers on the glaze and pigment of this bowl proved that this bowl was a product from a kiln in Gongxian county in Henan province fired in the Tang Dynasty, and the blue lines and patterns on the bowl were also painted with cobalt pigment. Therefore, the archaeological circles came to believe that the blue and white porcelain began to be fired during the Tang Dynasty. In the Yuan Dynasty, the achievements of color painting under the glaze from the Tang Dynasty were borrowed and inherited to make the blue and white porcelain technology more mature, and this helped establish a high historical status for the blue and white porcelain of the Yuan Dynasty.

For a long time, carving, the techniques of drawing and printing flower patterns on the surface decorations of various porcelains in China far exceeded the application of painting technique. After the firing and production of blue and white porcelain, the carving, drawing and printing techniques began to give way to the application of the painting technique. Therefore, the success in

A Yuan Dynasty porcelain jar unearthed at Baoding, Hebei Province.

the firing of blue and white porcelain was regarded as a milestone in the history of Chinese porcelain from monotonous color to the multi-colored porcelain, and an epoch-making progress in the porcelain-making history in China.

After the 1950s, archaeological excavations of the residential sites of the Yuan Dynasty, the kiln sites of the Yuan Dynasty and the tombs of the Yuan and Ming dynasties have unearthed a huge amount of the Yuan Dynasty white and blue porcelains. The most renowned findings include the blue and white porcelains unearthed from the ruins of the Dadu site in Beijing, including a blue and white flattened pot with phoenix pattern, which was perfectly shaped with perfect composition of paintings and perfect application of pigment and glaze, one blue and white vase imitating the ancient bronze ware, and one blue and white vessel. The blue and white porcelain jar with red flower glaze and lid unearthed from a kiln storage of the Yuan Dynasty in Baoding, Hebei province, and the blue and white porcelain with the painting of Xiao He chasing after Han Xin in the moonlight unearthed in Nanjing, Jiangsu province were all top-grade blue and white porcelains of the Yuan Dynasty.

The advantages of the blue and white porcelain of the Yuan Dynasty mainly include: the blue patterns are bright and the color is stable, because it is the color under the glaze, and the patterns will never fade away. More important, the white base and blue patterns of the blue and white porcelains give people a clean and elegant feeling, they are easy to wash and clean, and convey the artistic conception of the traditional Chinese ink and wash paintings. Therefore, the blue and white porcelain, since its birth, has been favored by Chinese and foreign porcelain lovers, and has become a unique Chinese porcelain renowned in the whole world.

# Painted Porcelain of the Ming-Qing Period

Blue flower porcelain objects are recognized as of the greatest artistic value among what is broadly referred to as "painted porcelain" of the Yuan, Ming and Qing dynasties. In producing such an object, pictures were drawn on the roughcast with a mineral paint rich in cobalt before the roughcast was coated with a kind of transparent glaze, and lines of the painting on the roughcast turned bright blue in the course of firing. In ancient times, cobalt-rich minerals were available in Yunnan, Zhejiang and Jiangxi provinces or imported from foreign lands. Not long after they came into being, blue flower porcelain objects grew popular enough to replace those with decorative designs cut, engraved or printed on roughcasts. Pictures bright blue against a pure white background produce the same artistic effect as traditional Chinese paintings done on paper. Jingdezhen in Jiangxi Province, known as China's "porcelain capital," has always been the best-known producer of blue flower porcelain.

Blue flower porcelain objects produced in the early 15th century are recognized as the best in quality and the most beautiful in design, and that period, as the heyday for this unique school of porcelain art. It is said that pictures on such objects were done with a mineral paint brought back from the Islamic world by Zheng He (1371 or 1375–1435). Pictures done with the paint, which has a high content of iron and a relatively low content of manganese, will be exceptionally bright, as bright as blue gems, provided temperature of the firing is properly controlled. Most pictures done on blue and white porcelain objects are flowers, the likes of peony, rose, camellia and chrysanthemum. Animal designs are mostly in the shape of dragons and phoenixes, as well as marine animals and unicorns. There are also pictures of fairies and pavilions and pictures depicting children playing games.

What is known to art historians as *dou cai* was developed during the Ming Dynasty. *Dou cai* objects are produced through firing at a relatively low temperature of about 800 degrees Centigrade, featuring pictures in outline done with blue paint on the roughcast and colorful pictures painted on the surface of the glaze by tracing the outlines beneath. The Chinese character *dou* means "struggle," and *cai*, "painting," the combination suggesting that pictures on the roughcast and the surface of the glaze "struggle" with each other for attention of the viewer.

The earliest *dou cai* objects were produced under the reign of Emperor Xuan De from 1426 to 1436. The best known *dou cai* products, however, were produced when Emperor Cheng Hua ruled China from 1465 to 1488. Pictures on Xuan De products are mostly red. In comparison, those on Cheng Hua products, mostly small in size such as wine cups, tea things and pots with lids, are bright with a variety of colors—red, blue, green, etc.

Another kind of porcelain objects of the Ming Dynasty were produced the same way as *dou cai*. The difference is that pictures on the surface of the glaze and those on the roughcast are independent

A Ming Dynasty porcelain jar.

A Qing Dynasty water jar.

of each other with complementing colors and designs.

Under the successive reigns under Emperors Kang Xi, Yong Zheng and Qian Long of the Qing Dynasty, painted enamel porcelain artifacts were for exclusive use by the imperial family living in the Forbidden City. These were produced in limited quantities right in the Forbidden City jointly by workmen and painters hired by the Imperial Household Affairs Office, with Jingdezhen, the "porcelain capital," supplying pure white porcelain ware on imperial order. Modern chemical analysis proves that cloisonne enamel used in production of painted enamel porcelain was not domestically available and therefore had to be imported.

Also during the Qing Dynasty, what is known to *fen cai* porcelain came into being as a development of painted porcelain and painted enamel porcelain. The Chinese character *fen* means "background" and *cai*, color, suggesting that painted pictures on a porcelain object have a white, bright red or green background made of glass powder to enhance the artistic effect through color

A Ming Dynasty porcelain kettle, with the spout, handle and lid button in the shape of dragons. It is a product of the Dehua Kilns.

contrast. Among *fen cai* products preserved to this day, those produced during the reign of Emperor Yong Zhong are recognized as the best in quality and design.

Beginning the early Ming Dynasty, porcelain production boomed in China and export of Chinese porcelain kept increasing as a result of Zheng He's voyages, reaching hundreds of thousands of pieces a year. In addition to Japan, Korea, Southeast Asia and other traditional markets, Chinese porcelain ware became popular in Europe, the Americas and Africa, where they were displayed, as treasures even more valuable than gold, in palaces of kings and residences of rich merchants and aristocrats. Likewise, routes on high seas for porcelain trading became known as the "Porcelain Road."

# Sculpture

# Tomb Figurines

According to *the Biography of Emperor Shi Huang of the Qin in the Historical Records*, right after the Qin Dynasty came to rule a unified China, the emperor ordered confiscation of all weapons in the hands of civilians as precaution against a possible rebellion. Confiscated weapons were sent to Xianyang, the national capital, for melting and, with the metal thus obtained, the emperor had 12 huge sculptures made to stand guard in front of his palace complex. The sculptures went missing when, after the emperor died, peasant rebel armies burned the palace complex to ruins. Despite that, large arrays of human figurines left over from the Qin and the following dynasties enable us to enjoy the unique beauty of ancient China's sculptural art.

Use of human figurines as funerary objects dates back to the Shang-Zhou period, to a period from 1600 BC to 1000 BC, to be exact. Before that period, hundreds and even more than 1,000 slaves were buried alive together with a dead nobleman, supposedly to serve their master in the nether world. The practice eventually ceased to exist as human labor became more and more productive and, as a result, human figurines were invented for use as funerary objects. Things of straw that look like scarecrows were used at first, followed by pottery and wooden figurines. Human figurines used as funerary objects before the Qin Dynasty were quite small, just a few to a dozen centimeters tall. Along with improvement in workmanship, however, they became more and more real in style, not only in human shape but also with details such as the hair, eyes and eyebrows painted. Some figurines "wear" armor suits painted in color, and we have also found figurines with silk clothes on. We are unable to know who invented the practice of using human figurines as funerary objects, but we do know that the practice originated from the late period of China's slavery society and thrived during the Qin and Han dynasties.

The Chinese sage Confucius was strongly against use of human figurines as funerary objects. Said he, "If only the originator of funerary figurines die without a son!" According to one assumption, even though the practice of burying people alive had ceased to exist, those figurines looked so real that they may prompt a desire to restore it and for that, the sage condemned its originator.

## Terracotta army guarding Emperor Shi Huang's tomb—a silent army array

In the year 246 BC, Ying Zheng, who was to become Emperor Shi Huang, was enthroned as king of the Qin State. Immediately after that, he ordered building of a tomb for himself even though he was only 13 years old. Construction of the tomb continued into the Qin Dynasty, of which Ying Zheng was the first emperor, and took 39 years to complete. Workmen in their hundreds of thousands were press-ganged for the task—more than 700,000 when the construction peaked. But not long after the emperor died and was buried in the tomb, peasant rebels overturned the dynasty and the superstructure of the tomb—in fact a palace complex—was burned to ashes. An earthen mound is what we can see of the tomb now.

One day in 1974, a farmer happened to dig into a burial pit near Emperor Shi Huang's tomb somewhere at Yanzhai Township, Lintong County near Xi'an, capital of Shaanxi Province. At a depth of about two meters, the farmer found a layer of red earth obviously having been baked in fire and, as he dug deeper, some pottery fragments and bronze weapons were unearthed. The farmer immediately stopped working, and reported what had happened to the proper authorities. Not long afterwards, large-scale excavation began in the area. Four burial pits were found, including one abandoned before its building was completed. The other three are underground structures of timber and earth. The No. 1 pit, with an area of 14,000 square meters, is the largest. The No. 2 pit, 6,000 square meters large, lies 20 meters to the north of the No. 1 pit, and takes the shape of a carpenter's square. The No. 3, in the shape of the Chinese character 凹, is the smallest. Altogether,

Many colored figurines were broken and discolored when they were unearthed. However, the vast majority had remnants of the original colors, and colors on some were largely intact.

more than 7,000 terracotta figures have been found in the pits along with 1,000 terracotta horses. Excavation of the site has been going on since 1974, bringing into daylight more and more relics.

The world was stunned by discovery of this huge terracotta army guarding the tomb of China's first emperor—one of the greatest wonders of ancient civilization. The site is a part of the Guanzhong Plain, the heartland of the northwest China Loess Highlands, where the earth, with pure, fine grains, is good for sculpturing. Painted pottery of the Yangshao Culture, a most outstanding representative of China's matriarchal civilization during its peak that dates to 5000 BC, originated from the area. Supply of earth was ensured and, moreover, producers of the terracotta figures were able to count on techniques for production of grey pottery that had become highly developed during the late Warring States Period. It is against this background that Emperor Shi Huang's terracotta army came into being.

Members of this "army" are life-like, their head, trunk plus the base averaging 1.8 meters in height. The different parts of a figure—the trunk, legs, arms, feet and hands—were produced separately and then assembled. The feet were installed on the base, then the legs on the feet, then the trunk on the feet, then the arms on the trunk, and the last step was to place the head on the neck.

Faces of the terracotta figures are typically of the Chinese living in north China—somewhat flat with narrow, long eyes and eyebrows, as well as prominent cheekbones. The eyebrows, eyes, noses, hair buns and moustaches were done manually, as were the finishing touches to the armor suits and clothes. Facial appearances and expressions are never the same, making the figures all the more life-like. Making of the mud roughcasts, large as they are, must be time consuming and call for strenuous human labor. The roughcasts were cured in fire in kilns, one or a few at a time, and the kilns should be near the tomb site.

The terracotta horses are life-like, too, and most of them are about 1.5 meters tall. They were produced the same way as the human figures. The horses, whether they are battle steeds or horses pulling the war chariots, all stand still. The saddles are of mud but the harnesses and bridles are real, with bronze fittings.

Here we are right at the excavation site, and greeting our eyes are those pottery warriors and horses grey in color, which look simple but magnificent. When these were buried, however, they were bright with colors painted on them—deep red, bright red, pink, light green, light purple, light blue, yellow, brown, as well as white, black and reddish brown. Of these colors, the most frequently used were deep red, pink, light green, light blue and reddish brown. Laboratory tests show that the colors were done with mineral paints, which were mixed with glue before they were applied. The color coatings have peeled off since it is such a long time since the terracotta figures were made and buried. When unearthed, some figures still had fragments of color and, from time to time, color fragments are found on nearby earth.

Once inside the Museum of Qin Dynasty Terracotta Warriors

Shown here is a bow man ready to shoot, which was unearthed from Pit No. 2.

and Battle Steeds, you'll find a huge army silent for well over 2,000 years. In No. 1 pit, there are 6,000 warriors standing in full attention, along with four wooden chariot models. These figurines are in neat formations, with 210 crossbow men in three columns serving as the vanguard. Behind the vanguard there are foot soldiers and chariots in 38 columns. Soldiers of the last column, facing the opposite direction, obviously serve as the rear guard. At either side of the columns there are soldiers protecting the flank. In the No. 2 pit we find 89 chariots driven by 356 horses, more than 900 foot

Photo shows Pit No. 1, which is 5 meters deep and has a weight-supporting wall every three meters. Some 1,000 terracotta warriors, horses and chariots have been unearthed from the pit.

soldiers and 116 battle steeds.

It is highly possible that these are real battle formations, and that armor suits "worn" by the warriors are imitations of real things. Foot soldiers "wear" short armor pieces, relative to those for their comrades on war chariots. Analysis of the designs leads to the conclusion that real soldiers must have armor pieces of animal hide. The horses all have their manes cut short and their tails tied, possibly to facilitate movement in real battles. Though not real, these terracotta warriors and horses bring history back to life. It is with this huge army that Emperor Shi Huang defeated the six states to the east of his kingdom and unified China, and the same "army" have stood guard for the emperor in the nether world.

Life-sized terracotta figures such as those found in Emperor Shi Huang's tomb in huge numbers had never been produced before

Here is an "entertainer" of the Eastern Han Dynasty, which was unearthed at Chengdu, Sichuan Province.

the Qin Dynasty and were not to be produced in the following dynasties. We may safely say that those terracotta figures supposedly guarding the emperor's tomb are unprecedented and unrepeatable. While serving as material evidence to the might of the dynasty, the magnitude of labor, financial and material resources used for their production brings to light the ruthlessness of the emperor, a most notorious dictator in the Chinese history.

## Figurines of the Han Dynasty—smaller but artistically better

The Qin Dynasty was short-lived, reigning for only 15 years. The country was thrown into chaos after the dynasty collapsed, with different peasant rebel groups fighting one another for supremacy, from which Liu Bang, leader of the most powerful group, emerged victor and made himself the first emperor of the Han Dynasty. The war-ravaged country was so poor that even the emperor himself had no way to have a chariot drawn by four horses of the same color as his status required. Ranking officials, on their part, had to use ox carts instead of horse chariots drawn by less than four horses, to which they would otherwise have been entitled. Given the destitution of the country and the people, it won't be difficult to understand why figurines of the Han Dynasty, though in huge numbers, are much smaller in size.

Terracotta figurines of the Han Dynasty have been unearthed from funerary pits near the tomb of Emperor Jing, the tomb belonging to Queen Dou of Emperor Wen, and the tomb of Emperor Xuan. Several thousand figurines have been excavated from the tomb of Emperor Jing, outnumbering those from the other tombs. Archeologists think that figurines buried to accompany these and other Han emperors and queens outnumber those terracotta figures from the tomb of Emperor Shi Huang. After all, the Han Dynasty ruled China for nearly 400 years, much longer than the Qin.

Terracotta figurines unearthed from the tomb of Emperor Jing are about 60 centimeters tall, those from the tomb of Queen Dou, 56 centimeters and those from the tomb of Emperor Xuan, 53Ñ57 centimeters. In all cases, Han Dynasty figurines are only one third as tall as those from the tomb of Emperor Shi Huang of the previous dynasty.

Though much smaller in size, Han Dynasty figurines are artistically better. Vivid facial expressions characterize those from the tomb of Emperor Jing. Figurines of maidservants from the tomb of Queen Dou, either standing or sitting, feature delicate lines characteristic of feminine beauty, unlike those from Emperor Shi Huang's tomb, of which most stand in rigid attention.

"Naked" figurines unearthed from a West Han tomb at Xi'an.

An "acrobatic troupe" of the Western Han Dynasty. The figurines were unearthed at Jinan, Shandong Province. A terracotta woman of the Western Han Dynasty. It was unearthed from an imperial tomb of the dynasty at Xi'an.

"Female cooks" of the Sui Dynasty. The pottery figurines were unearthed at Wuchang, Hubei Province.

Also worth mentioning are weapons and tools held by Han Dynasty figurine in their hands — spears, halberds, swords, crossbows and arrows, as well saws, adzes and chisels, all featuring excellent workmanship. These are made of either bronze or iron, and are about one third of the size of the real things. One figurine has a copper coin less than one centimeter in diameter. Small as it is, the two Chinese characters indicating its face value are clearly discernible.

Unlike those "warriors" guarding Emperor Shi Huang's tomb, figurines unearthed from Han Dynasty tombs are "naked," their physiological features clearly indicating whether they are men or women. Those unearthed from the tomb of Emperor Jing, numbering thousands, are, without exception, naked men. In recent years, naked female figurines have been found elsewhere.

The true fact is that these figurines were "born" naked. When they were buried, they had clothes or armor suits on, and these clothes and armor suits, all made of silk cloth, have perished due to decomposition over the centuries. Han Dynasty figurines used as funerary objects are without arms, but holes found below their shoulders suggest that they had wooden arms inserted which, too, have perished. Archeologists think that the original owners of these figurines wanted to have them produced as life-like as possible. These figurines, after all, were meant to serve them in the nether world.

Dancing, singing and story-telling figurines, wooden or pottery, have been unearthed from tombs dating to the mid- and late-Han Dynasty period, during which the dynasty, after a period of chaos, was able to enjoy a political stability and economic prosperity. The most fascinating, most life-like are those wooden entertainers unearthed from some late-Han Dynasty tombs in Yutai and Yangzhou areas under the jurisdiction of Jiangsu Province, east China.

From a Western Han Dynasty tomb on Mt. Wuying near Jinan, the capital city of Shandong Province, archeologists have found a group of two dozen figurines. These include six performers, seven musicians beating a drum, striking musical chimes and playing pluck and other instruments, as well as a man clothed in red who seems to be the conductor of the orchestra. Of the six performers, two women are dancing, their long sleeves waving and swirling, while the four men, in short jackets and barefooted, are doing acrobatics—throwing somersaults, standing on the hands and doing jujitsu. The performers and musicians are placed on a board, and beyond the board are "spectators."

In addition to entertainers, archeologists have unearthed from sites in Henan Province figurines featuring workmen winnowing rice husks or husking rice with mortar and pestle, as well as models of cattle, sheep, chickens, dogs, geese and pigs.

## The splendid tri-color glazed pottery figures of the Tang Dynasty

From the third century AD to the sixth, China was first divided, then reunified and then divided again. The country was first divided into three kingdoms that kept fighting one another, until the Wei overturned the other two and made itself the Wei Dynasty. But, before long, the Wei was replaced by a new dynasty called Jin. After the Jin collapsed, there emerged four dynasties that took control of the areas south of the Yangtze River in succession and five, also in succession, of the areas north of the river, which are collectively known as the "Southern and Northern Dynasties."

Huge changes took place during this period in production techniques and artistic style of pottery figures. Funerary pottery figures unearthed from tombs of the Western Jin Dynasty (265–317) fall into four categories. A tomb of this period invariably has, in front of its gate, a bull-like animal with upright horns and warriors in armor suits supposedly to ward off invasion by evil spirits. Inside the tomb there are ox carts and horses meant for use by the tomb owner in the nether world, along with male and female attendants, as well as kitchen utensils, water wells, grinding mills and domestic animals and poultry. Wars were fought one after

A tri-color pottery maidservant of the Tang Dynasty. It was unearthed at Xi'an, Shaanxi Province.

A pottery warrior guarding a Tang Dynasty tomb at Liquan, Shaanxi Province.

This tri-color pottery figurine of the Tang Dynasty obviously features a man from central or western Asia.

another between warlords during the period of the Southern and Northern Dynasties (420–589). To protect themselves and the areas under their influence, members of the land gentry often had their plantations rebuilt into castles and set up private armies. That may explain why archeologists have found, in tombs of that period, pottery guards and cavalrymen in neat columns.

China's feudal society had its heyday under the Tang Dynasty (618–907), and funerary objects of the Tang Dynasty, especially those built when Emperor Gao Zong and Empress Wu Zetian reigned supreme, mirror the dynasty's economic prosperity and military might, as well as peace and political stability the dynasty was able to enjoy. Legendary animal figures supposedly to protect tomb owners were gone, and in their place were fierce-looking guardian gods with animal figures underfoot. Also found in Tang tombs are figurines of civil and military officials in formal attire. Colorful steeds replaced ox carts in tombs of the long period from the Southern and Northern Dynasties to the Sui, the immediately proceeding dynasty. Also gone were those "private armies." From Tang tombs archeologists have found jubilant horse-riding hunters and musicians, as well as polo players.

The dynasty gave birth to tri-color glazed pottery figurines, which are recognized as representing the peak of ancient Chinese pottery sculptural art. Production of such figurines calls for a temperature ranging from 800 to 1,100 degrees C. to ensure that colors of the glaze are bright but not transparent. Yellow, green and brown are the main colors, hence the "tri-

Picture shows an orchestra on camelback, which was unearthed from a Tang Dynasty tomb at Xi'an.

A tri-color pottery horse of the Tang Dynasty.

color glazed pottery figurines." Supplementary colors include blue and black.

As an art form, tri-color glazed pottery figures peaked under Emperor Xuan Zong, who happened to be an art lover and a womanizer at the same time and, probably under his influence, extravagance and wastefulness characterized the lifestyle under his reign. Female figurins produced during this period invariably have chubby faces and are in well filled-out shapes, with high hair buns, long skirts and composed facial expressions.

Nevertheless, even better known are tri-color pottery steeds produced during the Tang Dynasty. The four steeds unearthed from a tomb built in the year 723 for General Xianyu Tinghai are recognized as the most beautiful. These animals are all more than 50 centimeters tall. Two of them are white and the other two, yellow with white hooves, as well as white stripes round their long necks. The saddles and bridles are colorful with decorative patterns of golden flowers and leaves. Two of the horses have on their manes a three-flower pattern popular at the time, and the manes of the other two each bear a single pattern.

Another master piece unearthed from the same tomb is a camel carrying four musicians and a dancer on its back, the dancer, in green costumes, obviously belonging to an ethnic minority group of China's.

## Funerary figurines of the following dynasties

Funerary practices popular during the Tang Dynasty continued into the period from 907 to 960, when separatist regimes, known as the "five dynasties and ten kingdoms," were set up in different parts of China. Large numbers of pottery figurines have been unearthed from tombs of kings of local regimes and their officials. While assuming roughly the same style as figurines of the Tang Dynasty, these invariably have local characteristics. From a tomb of the Southern Tang regime on Mt. Niushou in Jiangning, Jiangsu Province, archeologists have found more than 200 pottery figurines even though the tomb were already robbed. Among these, some look strange—for example, fish and snakes with human heads and snakes with two heads, which could be guardians of the tomb.

China became unified again under the Song Dynasty (960–1279) and, by that time, funerary practices had changed a lot. Paper money and paper figures with skeletons of thin bamboo strips were burned in honor of the dead, replacing the use of pottery and wooden figurines buried alongside the dead. Despite that, archeologists have still been able to find figurines used as funerary objects, including some that are of great historic and cultural value. A whole array of stone figures has been unearthed from a Song tomb at Yandian, Henan Province. China's "porcelain capital," Jingdezhen of Jiangxi Province, became known for a number of porcelain entertainers unearthed from one of the tombs that date back to the same dynasty. It is interesting to note that pottery figurines have also been found in tombs of the Liao and Jin dynasties, which were ethnic minority political regimes existing side by side with the Song that ruled the main parts of the country. Two pottery figurines, one male and the other female, unearthed from a Liao tomb at Changping under Beijing's jurisdiction have a hairstyle typical of the Qidan (Khitan) ethnic group. From a tomb built in 1210 under the Jin regime archeologists have found painted figurines in the shape of actors and actresses, which are recognized for their importance to study of the ancient Chinese drama.

The Yuan Dynasty (1271–1368) set up by the Mongols succeeded the Song to rule China. Pottery figurines in large numbers have been unearthed from Yuan tombs in Shaanxi and Gansu provinces, which serve as material evidence to study of Mongol costumes. But archeologists are not sure whether funerary figures can be found in tombs of Mongol aristocrats.

During the succeeding Ming Dynasty (1368–1644), use of funerary figurines in large numbers again became symbol of the statues of the dead. Archeologists have unearthed beautiful wooden, pottery and glazed pottery figurines from tombs of Ming Dynasty princes in Jiangxi, Shandong and Sichuan provinces. Just from the tomb built in 1410 for the eldest son of Prince Zhu Yue more than 500 glazed pottery figurines were excavated. These form a guard of honor, its members surrounding a carriage drawn by an elephant. There must be even more figurines in tombs of the dynasty's emperors. Of the Thirteen Imperial Tombs of the Ming Dynasty in Beijing, one, belonging to Emperor Wan Li, has been excavated. From inside those huge trunks flanking the

**Thirteen Imperial Tombs of the Ming Dynasty**
The Ming Tombs, totaling 13, were a group of tombs where emperors of the Ming Dynasty were buried. The tombs are located at Mount Tianshou at the slope of the Yanshan Mountains in Changping District in the northwestern suburb of Beijing. At this site, in more than 230 years from the seventh year of Emperor Yongle of the Ming Dynasty (1409) when the Changling Tomb was built to the burial of the last emperor of the Ming Dynasty, Emperor Chongzhen, in the Siling Tomb, a total of 13 tombs for the emperors were constructed, seven tombs for concubines and one tomb for eunuch were also built. At this place, 13 emperors, 24 empresses, two princess and more than 30 concubines and one eunuch were buried.

emperor's coffin in the back chamber of the underground palace, archeologists found seven smaller trunks full of funerary figurines. Of these, six had perished along with the figurines in them. In the only one still in fair conditions, about 1,000 figurines were counted, including 248 that remained good enough to be taken out. These figurines, made of poplar, spruce or pine timber, all stand at attention and have beautifully painted eyes, eyebrows and lips. There could be nearly 10,000 figurines in all the smaller trunks.

It is not known whether use of funerary figurines was an institutional rule in the Qing Dynasty (1644–1911). From the tomb of General Wu Liuqi who lived in the early period of the dynasty, however, a group of pottery attendants has been excavated, along with pottery models of furniture. These are the most recent of all ancient Chinese funeral figurines unearthed so far.

# Mausoleum Sculptures of Stone

Mausoleum art objects of stone are monuments dedicated to the dead. Of these, the most frequently seen are watchtowers, tablets and statues placed in front of a mausoleum and at the either side of the road leading to its gate. Watchtowers placed in front of mausoleums originated from those placed in front of palace complexes to highlight the powers of the monarchs, which came to be used by high-class people as symbols of status during the Han Dynasty. Stone tablets came late, relative to stone watchtowers. Stone statues, however, are regarded as representing the highest artistic value among all mausoleum stone objects found in China. Legend goes that a giant named Wengzhong, ten meters tall and his foot print measuring two meters long, was seen shortly after Emperor Shi Huang unified China. Inspired, the emperor ordered confiscation of all weapons not in the hands of his government and, with the metal thus collected, he had a huge statue made and named it after the legendary giant. During the period of the Southern and Northern Dynasties (420–589), use of stone statues in front of tombs and mausoleums became a funerary practice. The practice was to be passed on, and stone statues in front of tombs or mausoleums continued to be called Wengzhong even though they are much smaller.

## Stone statues of the Han Dynasty

Those placed in front of the tomb of General Huo Qubing (140–117 BC) in what is now Xi'an, Shaanxi Province, are the most representative of stone statues left over from the Han Dynasty. Intelligent and courageous, the general distinguished himself in battles against nomads known as the Xiongnu, or Huns, who often crossed the northern borders to loot and kill during the early period of the dynasty. After the general died, he was buried near the capital on order of Emperor Wudi. The funeral was grand enough to suit his contribution to stability of the new dynasty, during which troops, clad in black armor suits, stood in full attention to pay their last respect to their dead commander. To ensure that the general's heroic deeds would be remembered forever, the tomb site was transformed in such a way as to assume the topographical features of the Qilian Mountains in northwest China, where imperial troops under his command fought the decisive battle and won. The earthen mound with the dead general buried beneath looked like a huge hill, and numerous stone animal figures were placed in front of the mound and on its slope. The exact number of such stone figures is unknown, and so is the exact location of each. Anyway, sixteen have survived erosion by nature over the past two milleniums, which are now kept in a museum set up by the local government. Most of these are 1.5 meters long, and the largest is 2.5 meters in length.

Among the animal statues we find a crouching horse, a leaping horse and a horse with a Hun under one of its hoofs. These may well be the theme statues, symbolic of the three stages of the war fought under the general's direction—preparations for the war, the battles fought and the final victory. The crouching horse seems on alert, ready to jump up for battle. The leaping horse impresses the viewer with might and resolve. The third horse stands firm as the bearded human figure beneath its hoof struggles to get free by trying to stab its belly with a spear.

Among other statues we find a crouching tiger, a crouching pig, a crouching bull, a sheep, an elephant and a fish. There is also a statue featuring a ferocious-looking legendary animal eating a sheep. Another statue features a man jostling with a bear.

Seen from an artistic point of view, those stone statues dedicated to Huo Qubing are quite crude. The traditional carving techniques were still in an early stage of development and cutting, carving and chiseling tools were primitive. More often than not, sculptural artists had to make do with the shape of the stone material with which they were going to produce a statue. In other words, they had to use the kind of stone material resembling, in shape, the statue they planned to make, so that carving and chiseling would be reduced as far as possible. They would, first of all, process the stone material and make it roughly resemble the planned statue and then concentrate on the most striking parts, the head, for example. For details, they had to resort to techniques of bas-relief and line cutting. Most statues were deliberately made crouch with the legs withheld from view in order to minimize the cutting.

## Stone statues of the Southern Dynasties

The Southern Dynasties refer to the four political regimes that once ruled areas south of the Yangtze River in succession, namely, the Song (420–479), Qi (479–502), Liang (502–557) and Chen (557–589). All of them had Nanjing as capital. By stone statues of the Southern Dynasties, we mean those animal statues placed in front of mausoleums and tombs belonging to emperors, princes and ranking officials of this period. Most such statues are found at sites in Nanjing as well as in Danyang and Jurong nearby, including 17 sites in Nanjing and 13 in Danyang that are now under state-level production.

Animal statues produced during the first few decades of the

Picture shows a fierce-looking legendary animal guarding the tomb of Emperor Xiao Jing of the Liang, one of the Southern Dynasties.

Southern Dynasties period look slightly crude while featuring a natural, primitive beauty. Those produced under the Qi and Liang dynasties, however, look much more lively and mighty. In comparison, statues of the Chen Dynasty look feeble, mirroring the decline of the regime.

Stone animal statues placed in front of mausoleums and tombs of the Southern Dynasties period are invariably in pairs, and also found are stone columns flanking the road leading to their gates, as well as stone tablets dedicated to the occupiers of the mausoleums and tombs. They look mighty and fierce, with full—fledged wings carved on their shoulders. Those placed in front of imperial tombs have double or single horns. Stone animal statues dedicated to princes and ranking officials are without horns. In whatever shape and with whatever name, these were regarded as auspicious animals.

There are scholars who link winged animal figures found in China to civilizations of ancient West Asia or North Africa. The author, however, holds that they are purely Chinese. Far back in the Warring States Period (475–221 BC), animal figures with wings were already produced. A most striking example is a stone animal statue inlaid with wings of gold and silver thread, which is a part of the tomb for Prince Zhong Shan of the Warring States Period. During the Han Dynasty, animal statues with wings were placed at either side of the road leading to a mausoleum or tomb, and were given such names as *tianlu* (heavenly blessing) and *bixie* (warding off the evil). A pair of stone animal statues of the Eastern Han Southern Dynasty are a case in point. The statues, which were unearthed in Luoyang City, Henan Province, each have a pair of wings on their shoulders. Stone statues of the Southern Dynasties period are more delicate in design and workmanship, representing progress achieved by the Chinese since the Han Dynasty in sculptural art.

## Stone statues of the Tang and Song dynasties

Most emperors of the Tang Dynasty (618–907) were buried near the capital, Chang'an or what is now Xi'an. To be exact, 18 imperial

A horse and its tamer in front of the tomb shared by Emperor Li Zhi of the Tang Dynasty and his queen, Empress Wu Zetian.

tombs of the dynasty are counted in a 100 kilometer-long area in the north part of the Guanzhong Basin, Shaanxi Province, which encompasses Qianxian, Lixian, Jingyang, Sanyuan, Fuping and Pucheng counties. Most of the tombs have hills behind, with neat groups of stone statues placed at either side of the roads leading to their main gates and beyond each side gates. Those flanking the so-called "divine roads" are the most magnificent—in fact regarded as the gem of the dynasty's sculptural art.

The indomitable will of the dynasty's founding fathers to seize control of China and consolidate their rule was the dominating theme of stone art works produced during the early period of the dynasty. The most representative of such works is a group of large-sized stone relieves that bring back to life the six battle steeds most favored by Li Shimin, the second emperor of the dynasty who reigned supreme from 627 to 649. As commander-in-chief of the Tang army, Li Shimin had played a pivotal role in wars that ushered in the birth of the Tang Dynasty.

"Guard of honor" in front of a Song Dynasty imperial tomb in Gongxian County, Henan Province.

The relieves are in a style of realism, with minute details depicting the might and grandeur of the horses including wounds caused by arrows on some of them. One of the horses is seen with a warrior standing in its front, trying to pull out an arrow shot deep into its body. The relieves were obviously meant to eulogize Emperor Li Shimin for his heroism. Though not seen with any of the horses, for such powerful portrayal of his battle steeds the emperor makes his presence in the mind's eye of the viewer.

Now let us see those stone statues placed in front of the tomb shared by Emperor Li Zhi, who reigned from 650 to 683, and his queen, Wu Zetian. These are regarded as more artistically sophisticated than those produced earlier. It may be interesting to note that by skillfully using political intrigues, Wu Zetian broke the normal line of succession for the imperial crown and was able to rule the country from 684 to 704. She was the sole female sovereign in the Chinese history.

The four gates of the mausoleum compound each have a pair of stone lions outside. In addition to stone lions, the north gate has six stone horses in its front. Flanking the "divine road" is an "imperial guard of honor" consisting complete arrays of stone statues. These comprise, from south to north in succession, a pair of columns that symbolize the imperial power, a pair of ostriches, a pair of horses with wings, five pairs of horses with a horse driver standing beside each, ten pairs of human figures and two pairs of stone tablets. There are also 61 statues of envoys from lands far away from China.

Relative to the six battle steeds, stone statues dedicated to Emperor Li Zhi and Empress Wu Zetian look composed and solemn. Horses, for example, all stand erect with their drivers.

By the time the Northern Song Dynasty (960–1127) ruled China, the system of centralized feudal monarchy that began with the Qin Dynasty had become firmly established. Shortly after the dynasty came into being, its imperial court promulgated a set of rigid rules on the design and construction of tombs for emperors and their queens, relatives of the imperial family and officials. These rules

Here is a "general" standing guard on the Divine Avenue leading to the main gate of the Thirteen Imperial Tombs of the Ming Dynasty.

also specified the number and size of the stone statues on the divine road leading to tombs for people of each rank. Under such rules, tombs of all Song Dynasty emperors are the same in design except some minor differences.

Stone statues dedicated to dead emperors of the Song Dynasty are more diverse in variety than those of the Tang Dynasty while assuming roughly the same artistic style. Elephants and elephant tamers, warriors in full armor suits, court attendants and Chinese unicorns are found among those stone statues placed in front of the Song Dynasty's imperial tombs. Moreover, use of statues in shapes of foreign envoys, sheep, tigers and auspicious birds became a must. There are 60 stone statues for each imperial tomb, which are placed at either side of the divine road except the stone lions guarding the east, west and north gates of the mausoleum compound. Statues along the divine road face each other across the road. They are placed south-north in order of stone columns, elephants and elephant tamers, auspicious birds, horses and horse drivers, tigers, sheep, foreign envoys, military officers, civil officials, lions guarding the south gate, warriors, stepping stones for horse riding, and court attendants. There are six foreign envoys in three pairs, and horses, tigers, sheep, military officers, civil officials, lions guarding the south gate, stepping stones and court attendants are in two pairs. All the human figures look respectful and submissive, as do the animal figures. These feature much better workmanship than their counterparts of the Tang Dynasty, with minute attention paid to details.

Royal tombs of the Liao and Xixia dynasties, which existed alongside the Song, also had stone statues in front of them, but none of them has survived to our time. Excavation of a Xixia royal tomb in Yinchuan, capital of Ningxia Hui Autonomous Region, resulted in discovery of the bases for some statues that were once there. Basing on the discovery, archeologists have concluded that there should have been about 30 stone statues in front of each royal tomb of the Xixia regime.

## Stone statues of the Ming and Qing dynasties

Stone statues ceased to be used as imperial funerary objects under the Yuan Dynasty (1271–1368) that succeeded the Song to reign supreme over China. This funerary practice was, however, restored immediately after the Ming Dynasty (1368–1644) replaced the Yuan. In 1369, Zhu Yuanzhang, the founding emperor of the new dynasty, ordered construction, in his native place, Fengyang of Anhui Province, of a mausoleum for his parents with stone statues flanking the divine road. Stone statues of the Ming Dynasty that have survived to our time are found in Fengyang, Yutai of Jiangsu Province where ancestors of the imperial family were buried, Nanjing of Jiangsu where Zhu Yuanzhang was buried, and in Beijing that has the tombs of 13 Ming Dynasty emperors.

Picture shows the "guard of honor" in front of the tomb of Zhu Yuanzhang, the founding emperor of the Ming Dynasty, in Nanjing.

Whether human or animal figures, these look submissive and rigid, testifying to the strengthening of the centralized feudal monarchy under the Ming Dynasty.

The practice of placing stone statues in front of imperial tombs continued into the Qing Dynasty (1644–1911), the difference being that those military and civil officials of stone "wear" uniforms in Manchurian style. The Qing, China's last feudal dynasty, was overturned in the 1911 Revolution. Even though the country was already republic, Yuan Shikai (1859–1916), a warlord careerist who maneuvered to presidency, attempted to bring China back to monarchy and made himself Emperor Hong Xian of China. His "dynasty," so to speak, survived for no more than three months before he abducted in frustration, amid nationwide protests and armed uprisings against him. Yuan died three months afterwards, and was buried in Anyang, Henan Province. The man had a group of stone statues built in front of his tomb, which look ugly with Western-style "military uniforms" on.

# Grotto Temples and Formative Art of Buddhism

Buddhism found its way into China about 2,000 years ago, during the Eastern Han Dynasty, rapidly spread during the period of the Wei-Jin-Southern-Northern dynasties, and peaked when the country was under the successive reign of Sui and Tang Dynasties. Digging of caves for Buddha worshipping was obviously inspired by cave temples that existed in the early stage of the religion's development in India.

## Clay sculptures in grotto temples

The Chinese began digging caves for worshipping of Buddhism in the third century AD. Such activities became popular from the fifth century to the eighth, and ceased to exist after the 16th century.

The so-called grotto art, which came into being along with digging of caves for Buddha worshipping, combines traditional Chinese architectural and sculptural arts and the art of mural painting. Grottoes that have survived to our time are found in Xinjiang, Gansu, Shaanxi, Shanxi, Henan, Hebei, Shandong, Sichuan and Yunnan. They differ from one another in style as natural conditions differ from place to place and also because they were dug at different times. The Korzer Grottoes in Baicheng, Xinjiang, and the Mogao Grottoes in Gansu are the oldest and largest in northwest China, and also the most outstanding representatives of ancient China's grotto art. Both are in Gobi deserts, where stone good enough for carving are hardly available. For this reason, murals and pained clay sculptures are the main art works in grottoes there.

The site of the Korzer Grottoes was a part of Guizi, one of the numerous ancient kingdoms in Central Asia, and artworks there are unique in both content and artistic style due to a strong influence of the Indian Buddhist art. The main structures include spacious cave halls where Buddhist sculptures are displayed for worshipping, as well as cave dwellings for resident Buddhists. Cave halls for worshipping are square or rectangular in shape with arched ceilings, and gates and windows are on the front walls. Buddhist sculptures for worshipping stand or sit in front of the back wall. There are grottoes with tunnels leading to the rear chambers where sculptures of the sleeping Buddha—Buddha after freedom from worldly existence—are placed on earthen platforms. Murals are found everywhere—on walls and ceilings of the halls, chambers and tunnels, and also on most

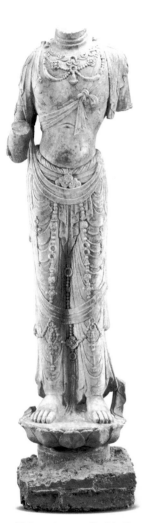

Picture shows a Bodhisattva statue of the Tang Dynasty. It is 163 centimeters tall.

Picture shows murals and painted sculptures in No. 329 grotto of Mogao, which were produced in the early Tang Dynasty.

parts of the walls of the rear chambers, telling stories about the life of Buddha and other Buddhist stories.

Buddhism kept spreading eastward, across Taklamakan Desert, the largest in China and the second largest in the world, in area next only to Sahara in Africa, and reached Dunhuang, a hub of communications on the ancient Silk Road and home to the world famous Mogao Grottoes. Also known as "Caves of a Thousand Buddha Sculptures," the Mogao Grottoes is the largest treasure house of clay sculptures and murals on Buddhist themes. Altogether, 493 caves are counted at Dunhuang, where murals that have survived to our time have a combined area of 45,000 square meters and painted clay sculptures exceed 2,400 in number. Back in 1900, a cave, nay, a treasure house with more than 40,000 cultural relics in it, was found by chance, and these include hand-written Buddhist scripts, documents and Buddhist paintings of around the eighth century. The discovery stunned the world and, since then, scholars across the world have developed an independent academic discipline called the "Dunhuang studies."

A painted Bodhisattva clay statue left over from the Tang Dynasty, which is enshrined in Cave No. 194, one of the Mogao grottoes at Dunhuang. It is plump in shape and wears high hair buns and thin garments, reflecting the aesthetic taste prevalent at the time.

This Buddha statue in Cave No. 20 at Yungang is 13 meters high. It is valued for being representative of the Yungang grotto art.

The oldest grottoes at Dunhuang were dug in the mid-fourth century. Building of grottoes peaked from the fifth century to the eighth, and began to decline after the 12th century.

The earliest painted clay sculptures in Mogao are often seen in groups of three, with Buddha in the company of two Bodhisattvas or Buddhist goddesses. Those left over from the Sui-Tang period, however, are mostly in groups of seven or nine, consisting of Buddhist gods, goddesses and guardians. Those life-like Buddhist goddesses and guardians are Chinese in everything—their physiques, clothes and facial looks, suggesting that Buddhism, an alien religion, had become an indispensable part of the Chinese culture.

### Stone statues in ancient grottoes

Like murals and painted clay sculptures in Korzer and Mogao grottoes, grotto stone statues in Yungang of Datong, Shanxi Province, and Longmen of Luoyang, Henan Province, are recognized as the most outstanding achievements in China's grotto art.

Grottoes with stone statues inside were mostly built during the period of the Northern Dynasties as imperial shrines for worshipping of Buddhism. The main statues in some grottoes at Yungang and Longmen are modeled after emperors who financed their building. Emperor Wen Cheng of the Northern Wei Dynasty, a devoted follower of Buddhism, had black birthmarks. It is not accidental that black "birthmarks" are found on the body of the main Buddha statue. Statues in the Binyang Cave at Longmen were built under the auspices of Emperor Wen Di of Northern Wei, and those in caves at Gongxian County, Henan Province, under Emperor Xuan Di of the same dynasty. In both caves there are beautifully carved relieves depicting the emperors and their wives and concubines attending Buddha worshipping ceremonies. It is said that the remains of Gao Huan, the founding emperor of the Northern Qi Dynasty, are kept in one of caves on Mt. Xiangtang near Linzhang County, Hebei Province. Empress Wu Zetian of the Tang Dynasty financed the building of a giant Buddha statue in Fengxian Temple, one of the cave temples at Longmen. According to historical records, the statues, which looks elegant and beautiful, was built with a donation of 20,000 strings of copper coins from her majesty's private coffer. It is, as a matter of fact, the very portrait of the empress. Grottoes left over from this period were built directly under the auspices of the monarchs. These were in fact state projects built with the best engineers and artists from all over the country, and the entire country's material and financial resources were pooled for their building, hence their huge size and surpassing artistic value.

The main Buddha statue in the cave dedicated to Emperor Gao Huan is 16.7 meters tall, its distance from the front wall of the cave being so short that for a full view of its face, viewers have to raise their heads and look up. This, plus the way the ceiling of the cave is designed, holds them in awe. The ears of the statue are long enough to reach the shoulders, and it has a chubby face and a straight nose. The kasaya—the outer vestment for a Buddhist monk—is worn across the left shoulder, with the right part of the statue's chest exposed. It is alien in style, in terms of its design and

Fengxian Temple is the largest open-air Buddhist shrine at Longmen. Building of the cave temple was completed in 675. This Buddha statue is 17.14 meters high and is rated as a best piece of China's grotto art.

the carving techniques.

Statues in Longmen Grottoes are strikingly different in facial looks from those in Yungang Grottoes, as the former came about half of a century later than the former. Statues of Buddhist gods and goddesses there look more Chinese, with long robes and tall hats popular among Han Chinese officials and aristocrats of the Southern Dynasties. Those "dressed" in such a way can be found among statues built during the second phase building of the Yungang Grottoes under Emperor Xiao Wen of the Northern Wei Dynasty, and even more are seen among statues in the Longmen Grottoes. Longmen statues built after the Northern Wei Dynasty have good shapes, with facial looks more human-like and clothes more delicately carved and, therefore, they look more elegant. Thanks to improvement in carving techniques, these are dignified while beautiful, different in artistic style from those in the Yungang Grottoes that feature a beauty of simplicity. These changes testify to success of a policy implemented under Emperor Xiao Wen of the Northern Wei Dynasty that encouraged absorption of the kind of culture popular in better developed southern China. This came after the dynasty moved its capital to Luoyang in the south. And this cultural assimilation culminated in a mainstream Buddhist art with statues in southern China style as the most prominent representatives. To sum up, Longmen statues played a pivotal role in the development of China's grotto art by connecting what had been achieved and what was to be achieved.

Grottoes of the Northern Qi Dynasty, as represented by those on Mt. Xiangtang in Handan, Hebei Province, and those on Mt. Tianlong in Shanxi, pushed China's grotto art to a new high. Buddhism was made the state religion by Northern Qi rulers headed by Gao Huan and Gao Yang in succession, who spared no effort to promote the religion. Buddhist shrines were built under their personal auspices. Eminent monks were invited to serve as "teachers of the state." Under imperial orders, all the queens and imperial concubines became lay Buddhists. The entire country's resources were pooled to build grottoes for Buddha worshipping on Mt. Xiangtang in what is now Handan, Hebei, and Mt. Tianlong in what is now Taiyuan, Shanxi. As some historical records put it, statues there are "magnificent enough to stun not only human beings but also beings in the nether world." They feature an artistic sophistication, different from grotto statues at both Yungang and Longmen. They combine artistic simplicity and painstaking attention to details, in fact largely modeled after real persons in scale and, therefore, they look natural enough to bring back to life those upper class men and women who lived at the time. Equally beautiful are decorations carved on those statues—honeysuckle, lotus and other flowers, for example.

Grottoes on Mt. Xiangtang are famous not only for those statues in them but also for stone corridors in front of them, which resemble structures of the same kind built with timber and bricks. The top of a stone corridor invariably takes the shape of a Buddhist pagoda in Indian style, which looks like a large bowl placed upside down. Flowers and leaves are carved on the pagoda, amid which there stands a legendary bird with gold wings. In short, grotto structures on Mt. Xiangtang are unique in every aspect, designed and built in such a way as to highlight local characteristics and characteristics of the times.

It is worthwhile to mention that grotto statues found in China were painted like murals and clay sculptures. The paints on most statues have peeled off due to erosion, but flakes of color are still discernible on some.

## Moveable Buddhist art objects of stone

Side by side with grotto artworks came removable artworks of stone kept in temples and inside pagodas for worshipping—mostly relieves of Buddhist images and inscriptions carved on stone cylinders and tablets. Such artworks have been unearthed in large quantities in both northern and southern China, mainly from beneath ruins of deserted temples and pagodas where they are placed in neat order. This prompts the guess that they were buried for protection when the religion was suppressed as it did occur from time to time. In northern China, Xiude Temple in Quyang County, Hebei Province, has the largest collection of stone Buddhist statues and these were built over a period longer than any other collection found so far in China. Stone statues of the Northern Dynasties in Qingzhou City, Shandong Province, are recognized as the artistically best. In southern China, the best known collection of ancient statues is kept in Wanfo Temple in Chengdu City, Sichuan Province.

More than 2,200 statues, partial or complete, have been unearthed from beneath Xiude Temple since the 1950s. These were produced during six successive periods beginning the fourth century and ending the tenth—the Northern Wei, Eastern Wei, Northern Qi, Sui, Tang and the Five Dynasties. Those left over from the Eastern Wei, Northern Qi and Sui dynasties outnumber those from the other dynasties, and most statues in the collection are small in size, carved on marble cylinders. Two factors may explain why mass production of marble statues was possible in the area. First, the area abounds in marble deposits and, second, by the mid-fourth century, what is now Hebei Province had become a center of Buddhism in China. Most of the Northern Wei statues in the temple's collection present Maitreya, a Bodhisattva, as a very stout monk cross-legged and with a broad smile on his face and his breast and punch exposed to view. There are far fewer statues of Maitreya among statues of the East Wei Dynasty and, in comparison, large numbers of statues presenting Avalokitesvara, the Goddess of Mercy, are found in the collection. Statues of Amitabha, the God of Infinite Quantities, and Amitayus, the God of Eternal Life, are found among statues of the Northern Qi Dynasty. Statues of the Eastern Wei Dynasty feature delicate lines, different from those of the Northern Wei Dynasty reputed for hard, straight lines. Those of the Northern Qi look even more natural with amiable facial expressions, in an artistic style that also characterize those lively, plump statues of the Tang Dynasty. Stone

Stone Buddha statue at Xinglong Temple in Qingzhou, Shandong Province. It was produced during the Northern Dynasties.

Stone Bodhisattva statue at Xinglong Temple in Qingzhou, Shandong Province. It was produced during the late Northern Dynasties.

statues of the Northern Dynasties were unearthed in batches from ruins in the Qingzhou area, Shandong Province, from the 1970s to the 1990s. Excavation of more than 400 statues in one batch, along with fragments and heads that had fallen from statues, stunned the world. These roughly fall into four categories according to their artistic styles and the inscriptions on them that indicate the time of their production—those of the late Northern Wei, those of the early Eastern Wei, those of the late Eastern Wei, and those of the Northern Qi. Those produced in the period spanning from the late Northern Wei to the early Eastern Wei often present one Buddha and two Bodhisattvas together against a screen that takes the shape of a boat, "wearing" tall hats and large loose robes popular among scholars and officials in China's heartland. Significant changes are observed in statues of the late Eastern Wei and Northern Qi, as manifested in a sharp increase in the number of single Buddhist images. This is true especially to those of the Northern Qi. Buddhist

A Buddha statue built in the year 483, under the reign of the Qi, one of the Southern Dynasties.

statues presented as singles account for a vast majority of those produced under the dynasty. Instead of large, loose robes, tight-fit clothes, clothes without folds, constitute their most salient feature. In some cases, Buddhist vestments, formed with large blocks, are painted on statues, and within such blocks there are painted pictures telling Buddhist stories, and the images are presented as people from alien lands, immortals, as well as ghosts who stay hungry forever.

Far back in the 1880s, stone carvings were already unearthed from beneath Wanfo Temple in Chengdu, and in the 1990s, more were unearthed, bringing to more than 300 the total number of pieces found there. Most carvings are broken, but can still be identified as belonging to three of the Southern Dynasties, the Song, Qi and Liang, and to Northern Zhou, Sui and Tang dynasties. These are good enough to serve as material evidence to study of ancient Buddhist art in southern China, in Sichuan in particular. They are quite complicated in structure, often presenting a main Buddha together with attendants, as well as numerous other figures including divine guardians, the main Buddha's followers and, in some cases, even a group of six or eight entertainers. One produced in the year 547 presents the Goddess of Mercy with a floral crown on, standing gracefully in the middle. There is a lion at either side of the goddess, with an attendant riding on its back. Beyond the lions there are two elephants each carrying on its back a divine guardian. Below the goddess there is an orchestra of eight musicians playing pipe instruments. These figures are well distributed, with a clear distinction between the most important and lesser ones.

Most stone tablets with carved pictures on Buddhist themes are found in northern China, in Henan, Shaanxi and Shanxi, to be more exact. These are either flat or take the shape of a column with four sides, with pictures carved on each. Such pictures are similar to grotto statues in artistic style. They are not large due to limitation of the space, but because of that, they feature even better workmanship. Stone tablets invariably bear inscriptions that tell the reasons for their production, and the names, birthplaces and social status of the persons who sponsored their production. In some cases, the persons' images are carved along with such inscriptions.

## The decline of grotto temples

The Buddhist civilization came to extinction in India, the birthplace of the religion, with invasion of the Arabs in the 13th century, meaning that China lost a major source of inspiration for developing its own Buddhist culture. Historical records show that from the Yuan Dynasty to the mid-Ming period, there was sporadic production of cliff carvings and grotto statues. With a constant eastward shifting of the country's political and economic gravity, shipping eventually replaced the Silk Road which, starting in western China, had linked the country with countries and regions to its west. Under the Qing, China's last feudal dynasty, the Tibetan school of Buddhism was made the de facto state religion and, as a result, temple buildings and copper statues in Tibetan style became increasingly popular in the country's heartland. Grotto temples and art, once so brilliant, eventually ceased to develop.

# Painting

Beginning from the painting relics from the painted pottery of the Neolithic Age, the development of paintings in China has a history of several thousand years. Of all genres of paintings, the Chinese traditional painting is the most successful and has the far-reaching influence on the Chinese culture and arts. Chinese traditional painting, also known as Chinese painting, is an art of making paintings on specially-made rice paper or silk with brush, ink and paints. The genre can be divided into figure painting, landscape painting and flower-bird painting according to their themes; and can be divided into impressionistic (abstract) painting and fine brushwork painting according to the painting techniques. Prior to the maturity of the Chinese painting, Chinese painting was also done in the forms of rock painting, silk painting and mural painting.

# The Origin of the Art of Painting

Painted pottery images in the pre-history ages in China already indicated some information about primitive painting art. Of them, the "stork, fish and zax patterns" painted on a pottery jar of the Yangshao Culture, unearthed in Yancun village, Linru county in Henan province, is widely believed to be a pre-history painting work. At present, there is a lack of information about the painting relics from the Shang and Western Zhou dynasties. In the excavations of the Yin Ruins in Anyang, Henan province, red patterns and black dots were found on the remnants of white rammed earth from the buildings belonging to the late years of the Yin Dynasty, which formed symmetric patterns, and they indicated that the then buildings had already had colored murals.

In the Spring and Warring States Period, painting developed to a new level, and the typical works of this period were the two silk paintings unearthed from a Chu State tomb during the Warring States Period in Changsha, Hunan province. They are, to date, the earliest paintings ever found in China.

The two silk paintings are all in the form of rectangle, and all feature standing figures facing the left. In one of the two painting, a man, with tall hat and sword and with both hands holding the bridle, rides a dragon. Over the head of the man, there is a painted canopy. The dragon, with a perking head and raising tail, is shaped like a boat. At the tail of the dragon, there is a grey heron, and beneath the dragon, there are auspicious clouds and a carp swimming forward. The fringes of the canopy and the lacing below the man's chin are flying backwards, the body of

The silk painting *human driving dragon* unearthed from a Tomb of the Warring States Period in Changsha, Hunan Province.

the man leans backwards slightly, and the long bridle is held tight. All these form a vivid posture of marching forward rapidly.

The other silk paining depicts a woman in long dresses. Her hair is neatly tied at the back of the head, she holds her hands in front of the chest, her waist is slim and her sleeves are broad, and her dresses have beautiful patterns similar to silk products. The woman's face is perfectly drawn and shaped, with thin eyebrows and clear eyes, and she looks straightly ahead and her pose conveys something pious. Above the head of the woman, there is a marching phoenix-like bird, with perking head, spread wings and beautifully-raised tail. In front of the woman, there is a swimming dragon, with its body in the shape of an "S" and with its head perking up towards the sky. The two silk paintings use the divine creatures as dragon and phoenix to imply the heaven for the dead, therefore, the paintings are something related to funeral ceremonies.

The silk paintings from the Chu State tomb already had some important attributes of Chinese traditional painting. First, lines were the base for the composition; second, within the outline formed by ink lines, the rendering technique appeared and was applied in addition to other color application techniques; third, the painting began to highlight the attributes of charm and vividness, and the silk paintings were very vivid in depicting figures, dragon, phoenix, birds and fish. All these show that by the Warring States Period, the development of Chinese traditional painting was in the key stage of transition from the bourgeoning period to maturity.

# Paintings of the Han and Jin Dynasties

A folk story goes like this: Wang Zhaojun, popularly regarded as one of the four ancient beauties in the Chinese history, did not bribe the imperial court painter Mao Yanshou, so she was drawn as an ugly woman and was ultimately selected and sent to marry a the Hun for peace between the Han and the Hun. The marriage between Wang Zhaojun and a Hun led to a historic achievement of peace for nearly half a century, and this is a fact accepted historians. However, whether or not the story conformed to historical facts is

Stone carvings unearthed from a tomb of the Han Dynasty at Xuzhou, Jiangsu Province.

A copy of Gu Kaizhi's *Nymph of the Luo River*, collected by Beijing Palace Museum.

still subject to disagreement even today. But it, at least, indicated that the figure painting had already reached a developed stage in the Han Dynasty. The painter in this story, Mao Yanshou, was a true historical figure, according to historical records, and was a well-established painter. It is said that he could "truthfully draw portraits of the old, the young, the beautiful and the ugly."

Of the Han paintings, the stone sculpted painting of the Han Dynasty is worth mentioning. The Han stone sculpted painting is a kind of unique decorative arts for the tomb walls, and could be called "stone sculpture murals." It appeared in the late years of the Western Han Dynasty, primed later and lasted throughout the Eastern Han Dynasty. With the growing power and wealth of the imperial families and aristocrats, they developed a fad for extravagant burials. Therefore, they were no longer satisfied with the ink and wash paintings on the tomb walls, and began to apply the method of incorporating sculpture into painting in building tombs. This method paid greater attention to details, and the works so created could last longer or permanently.

In the production of the Han stone sculpted painting, the painters first drew drafts on the surface of the selected stone (usually flat and smooth stone), the stoneworkers chased and chisel according to the painting drafts, and then the painters would apply colors to the sculpted stone. Therefore, the overall artistic effect of the Han stone sculpted painting is more similar to paintings rather than stone sculpture.

The Han stone sculpted painting usually depicted the daily life, social activities and activities for the purpose of production of the dead buried in the tombs. In addition, they also chose to apply such themes as primitive worshipping and the worshipping for the gods and the divine. These sculpted paintings were similar to murals engraved in the walls of the tombs, vividly depicted the prominent status of the dead before their death, their luxurious living and their worshipping of the ancestors, gods and the divine, and conveyed their desire for luxurious life in the afterworld and their desire for immortality.

The figure sculptures of the Han stone sculpted paintings usually showed the profile posture of the figures, and only a very few portraits were in the obverse posture, therefore, the rubbings made were usually in the form of silhouette. The composition of paintings usually applied the horizontal view along the base line. Under this technique, the images were completely arranged horizontally along the base line, in disregard of any depth or distance. At the same time, the entire stone surface was divided into several columns, with images in different columns standing as independent units and with different themes, and on some stone, as many as seven columns were designed on a single stone.

In the late years of the Eastern Han Dynasty, warlords were fighting for their own regimes and three confronting kingdoms were formed. Afterwards, a brief unification was realized in the Western Jin Dynasty, but a greater warring situation followed, and the Eastern Jin regime was established south of the Yangtze River. The wars and long-distant migration served as conditions for breaking the old barriers between the Han and Jin cultures, and the central culture and the intrinsic Sun-Wu culture existing south of the Yangtze River began to converge and new elements were incorporated into the cultures. The changes in cultures provided fertile soil for art creations. Therefore, the paintings of the Eastern Jin prospered, and famous painters as Dai Kui (348–409) and Gu

Kaizhi (326–369) emerged.

Gu Kaizhi had a far-reaching influence on the development of paintings. His works were admired by all, because he was innovative and could break the old patterns of figure paintings of the Han and the Wei dynasties. Therefore, Xie An (320–385) then spoke highly of him, saying that "his paintings were unprecedented." The most prominent characteristic of paintings by Gu Kaizhi was that his paintings not only stressed the "objects in the paintings," but also tried to achieve the goal of "perfect and vivid." Therefore, Zhang Yanyuan of the Tang Dynasty, in his "On Famous Paintings in History," commented on the application of the brush by Gu Kaizhi, saying that he "planned before applying the brush, continued to plan after completing the paintings." There are now three anthologies containing the imitations of paintings by Gu Kaizhi—*Admonitions of the Instructress to the Palace Ladies*, *Nymph of the Luo River* and *Wise and Benevolent Women*. The latter two anthologies were imitations done in the Song Dynasty, and are not truthful to the originals, and the first anthology contained imitations virtually truthful to the originals.

# Painting Style of the Sui-Tang Period

After the unification of the country in the Sui Dynasty, painters from across the country gathered in the then cultural center—the capital city Daxing (now Xi'an in Shaanxi province). This effectively broke the barriers between the north and the south, and between the east and the west, and painters of different schools and styles had the chance of convergence to exchange skills and learn from one another.

In the early years of the Tang Dynasty, the art of painting further prospered on the basis of achievements in the Sui Dynasty. In Changan, the capital city, there were two major schools of painting—the central style and the western style. The most typical painter of the central style was Yan Liben (601–673). The painting

*Imperial Carriage*, now collected by the Palace Museum in Beijing, is considered by many as a work by Yan Liben. The painting featured Emperor Taizong Li Shimin (reigned 627–649) of the Tang Dynasty meeting envoys from the Tubo. From this painting, the painter drew the figures with fine and meticulous brush, applied diversified lines, and tried to convey the figures' personality and state of mind through details. It is safe to say that this painting is "perfect and vivid." The painter continued the skills of blowing up the size the major figure and reducing the body sizes of the servants, which was widely used during the Northern and Southern Dynasty. In this painting, Emperor Taizhong, sitting in the imperial sedan, was obviously bigger than servant men and women, and the bodies of the figures in this painting were too high, somehow in disproportion.

The typical painter of the western style was Weichi Yiseng, the son of famous Sui Dynasty painter Weichi Bazhi, and was also named Junior Weichi. The main differences between the western and central styles of paintings were the application of the brush and the application of pigment. The works of Weichi Yiseng were powerful in

*Imperial Carriage*, attributed to Yan Liben of the Tang Dynasty, collected by Beijing Palace Museum.

A copy of Zhang Xuan's *Ladies of the Dukedom of Guo Going on a Spring Outing*, collected by Liaoning Museum.

the application of brush lines, he applied the painting skill of convexo-concave application of pigment, and he was good at producing a three-dimensional effect of the thick and thin application of colors. Unfortunately, none of his works is available now.

The development and evolution of paintings from the Sui Dynasty to the early Tang Dynasty helped lay a solid foundation for the prosperity of the art of painting in the Tang Dynasty. With the social and economic development in the Tang Dynasty, literature and arts developed to a new high in the prime time of the Tang Dynasty, and Wu Daozi (680–759), reputed as the "painting saint," was the outstanding representative of this era. Wu Daozi was an energetic and enthusiastic painter, had a superb ability in realism painting and memorization, and painted accurately and to the point. His paintings were known for their vigorous and powerful lines, vivid configuration, and were all "vivid, dynamic and true to life," and people often use the phrase "ribbons in Wu Daozi's painting bringing wind" to describe his paintings. Wu Daozi also abandoned the traditional "thick color" painting skills, and he sometimes even did not apply any color at all, known as "colorless paintings."

Of the figure and portrait paintings of the Tang Dynasty after Wu Daozi, the painters devoted most their time and efforts in producing works depicting the growing extravagant life of imperial court and aristocrats, in addition to paintings about the emperors, officials and religious figures, and they were especially fond of producing paintings of plumpy women as Yang Yuhuan, the imperial concubine. At that time, there were several painters known for their paintings of women, such as Zhang Xuan and Zhou Fang. The well-known paintings by Zhang Xuan include *Court Ladies Preparing Newly Woven Silk* and *Ladies of the Dukedom of Guo Going on a Spring Outing*, which are still imitated even today, and the famous works by

The fresco in Mogao Grottoes in Dunhuang, painted in the Tang Dynasty.

Zhou Fang include *Imperial Court Ladies with Silk Fans* and *Imperial Court Lady Tuning the Qin* and *Sipping the Tea*.

Mural also had an extremely important position in the creation of paintings in the Tang Dynasty. For a great number of famous painters including Wu Daozi, their major creation activities were to paint murals in the imperial palaces and temples. It is reported that in the palaces in Changan and Luoyang, there were more than 300 murals created and painted by Wu Daozi. However, the palaces and temples of the Tang Dynasty have been destroyed, and fortunately, some murals painted on the walls of tomb chambers are preserved. Although these murals were not done by famous painters, they were all skillfully painted. In particular, those murals in the imperial tombs near Changan should have been done by the then renowned painters and craftsmen. These murals all reflected the then social fads and the popular painting styles, and serve as precious materials for the study of the Tang Dynasty murals today.

Of the tomb murals in the Tang Dynasty, those murals in the tombs of princes and princesses represented the highest level of mural paintings at that time. These mural paintings highlighted to depict two major scenarios: first, the ceremonies indicating the status of the dead, and second, the male and female servants in the imperial court life. In the first scenario, it depicted the grand and extravagant scenes, and in the second scenario, it focused to depict the living styles of the imperial court and all figures in the murals were vivid and finely drawn. The single portraits and group portraits were all known as the masterpieces of the figure paintings of the Tang Dynasty.

# Painting Academy of the Song Dynasty

During the Song dynasties, the imperial courts set up the Hanlin Huayuan (Imperial Painting Academy). The academy was a pool of painters for the imperial court and was the painting creation center for the imperial courts, imperial families and aristocrats. Renowned painters from across the country gathered in the academy, lived on salary paid and guaranteed by the imperial court, enjoyed a stable and comfortable environment for artistic creations, had the opportunities to exchange with other painters and learn from one another and to learn the art of imperial court paintings, and had the convenience to further improve their skills. In the Song dynasties, the academy made great contributions to the prosperity of the painting art.

The painting academy in the Northern Song Dynasty developed to its peak level during the reign of Emperor Huizong Zhao Ji (reigned 1101–1125). Emperor Huizong was politically incapable of ruling the country, chose to trust those corrupt and incapable officials, and caused the Northern Song Dynasty to its demise. In the field of painting art, he demonstrated his talent and ability and could be considered a painter or a connoisseur of arts. Due to his personally hobby, Zhao Ji gave special emphasis to the development of the painting academy. At that time, the academy pooled the best talents from across the country, had such famous painters as Ma Bi, Zhang Zeduan (1085–1145), Fu Xie, Wang Ximeng (1096–?), Liu Zonggu, Su Hanchen and Zhu Rui, and could be considered the heyday of imperial court painting in the history of Chinese paintings. Zhao Ji was also good at painting and

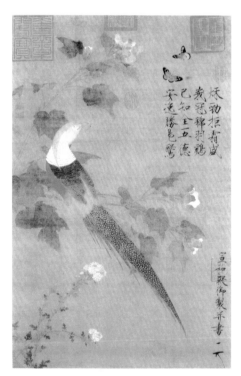

*Hibiscus and Golden Pheasant*, by Zhao Ji of the Song Dynasty, collected by Beijing Palace Museum.

calligraphy, and established his own calligraphic style of "slender golden style" in calligraphy, was good at drawing flower-bird, figure and landscape paintings, and pursued his unique ways of paintings and calligraphy. His masterpieces included the flower-bird painting *Hibiscus and Golden Pheasant* and *Auspicious Cranes*. He also created many figure paintings and landscape paintings, with *Listening to the Qin* as the most noteworthy.

In the Song dynasties, a big number of figure paintings featuring the ordinary people and their life were produced. These genre paintings chose to depict the everyday life of the common folks and civilians, themed on farming, weaving, vendors, children playing, transporting, acupuncture by village doctors and opera performance, and these activities were all vividly incorporated into the paintings. Some of the genre paintings incorporated figures in the landscape and building paintings to produce long-scroll panorama scenes. The most well-known of such paintings was *Along the River during the Qingming Festival* by Zhang Zeduan, which depicted the prosperous street scenes in Bianliang (now Kaifeng in Henan province), the then capital city. The scroll began with the scenes in the wild suburb to show the busy shipping scenes along the Bianhe River and bridges, and continued to depict the city gate and streets, and buildings as tea houses, bars, drugstores and temples, and incorporated as many as more than 500 different figures in this painting. This was a highly realistic masterpiece, and depicted the scenes and life in the capital city.

Landscape paintings had an important position in the paintings of the Song dynasties, and the painting composition and skills were also developed to a new level. In the early years of the Northern Song Dynasty, most of landscape paintings applied the panorama view of landscapes, and the most famous painters were Li Cheng (919–967) and Fan Kuan. Their works, while faithful in depicting the nature, were mainly done in ink and wash. However, their works were also different. Li Cheng, in his paintings, mainly chose the forests and desolate scenes, and Fan Kuan chose to paint the grand and imposing mountains.

Of the landscape painters in the Southern Song Dynasty (1127–1279), the most famous included Li Tang (1066–1150), Liu Songnian (1155–1218) Ma Yuan (1140–1225) and Xia Gui, and they were known as the four masters of the Southern Song Dynasty. Of them, Ma Yuan and Xia Gui had greater influence on the painting in the generations to come. They abandoned the panoramic composition of pictures, and boldly chose a corner or section of the mountains for their paintings and left wide white space in their works so as to highlight the beauty of the mountains and to give the viewers unlimited space for wild imagination, and they were therefore nicknamed "Ma, a corner of the mountain" and "Xia, a section of the mountain." This bold selection of landscapes for the paintings reflected the painters' favorites, the paintings were therefore beautiful and poetic, and they helped promote the creation of landscape paintings to a new height.

*Along the River during the Qingming Festival* (partial), by Zhang Zeduan of the Song Dynasty, collected by Beijing Palace Museum.

# The Literati Paintings in the Yuan, Ming and Qing Dynasties

The painting style in ancient China underwent a major change in the Yuan Dynasty, and this change was characterized by the emergence of "literati painting." The painting academy system, popular in the Song dynasties, was abandoned during the Yuan Dynasty. Some painters were still serving the imperial court, but they were no longer having much impact on the trends and the mainstream of the painting circles. The style of pursuing extravagance and grandness, advocated by the painting academy of the Song dynasties, was also no longer popular. Figure painting, which used to have a prominent position in the themes for ancient paintings in China, was also losing its glamour and was in decline. Literati paintings, created and represented by Su Shi (1037–1101)

*Lucid Mountains and Remote Streams*, by Xia Gui of the Song Dynasty, collected by Taibei Palace Museum.

and Mi Fu (1051–1107), became the mainstream. This school of painting advocated concise application of the painting brush and pursued the interesting forms of paintings. This style began to be favored among the literati who did not want to be officials in the Yuan Dynasty, and became the mainstream of the painting circles in the Yuan Dynasty. They used painting as a way to show their mood and emotion, paid little attention to realistic features while drawing the paintings, and tried to make their paintings simple and natural. They usually chose mountains and water as the theme to express themselves, also often chose the withered trees or rocks as their painting themes, or plum, orchid, bamboo and chrysanthemum among other flowers as their themes.

The literati painting of the Yuan Dynasty was the medium of the painters to express their thought and emotion, and what was shown in the paintings usually indicated the painters' pursuit. Sometimes, however, the painters still felt that the paintings were insufficient to express themselves, and then chose other forms of arts to achieve their goals. These literati painters were usually highly accomplished in literature and were good at calligraphy, they would then choose to write poems on the painting to further express themselves, and subsequently, made their paintings more beautiful. In addition to writing poems on their paintings, they also chose to indicate their intentions for doing the paintings, or wrote improvisational postscript on the paintings and then applied their seals on them. By doing so, the works became a combination of painting, inscription and seal, and became a new type of paintings by literati painters. This meant changes to the traditional features of the Chinese paintings, and had a far-reaching significance on the paintings in the Ming and Qing dynasties.

The Wumen Painting School of painters of the Ming Dynasty, represented by Shen Zhou (1427–1509) Wen Zhengming (1470–1559), Tang Yin (1470–1523) and Chou Ying (1509–1551), the Four Monk Painters of the Qing Dynasty represented by Shi Tao (1630–1724) and Zhu Da (1626–1705), and the Eight Eccentrics of Yangzhou represented by Zheng Banqiao (1693–1765)

**Wumen Painting School**
In the Ming Dynasty, the Suzhou region south of the Yangtze River became a pool of literati. According to historical records, there were more than 150 painters in Suzhou then, accounting for one-fifth of the total in the Ming Dynasty. They formed an powerful and influential school of painters. Because Suzhou was called "Wumen" in history, this was therefore named the "Wumen Painting School." The Wumen Painting School emphasized to carry forward the traditional skills of the predecessors, highlighted the charms and expressions of their works, and their skills, techniques and creations had great influence on the painters in the generations to come.

*Dwelling in the Fuchun Mountains*, by Huang Gongwang of the Yuan Dynasty.

*Peony and Rocks*, by Xu Wei of the Ming Dynasty.

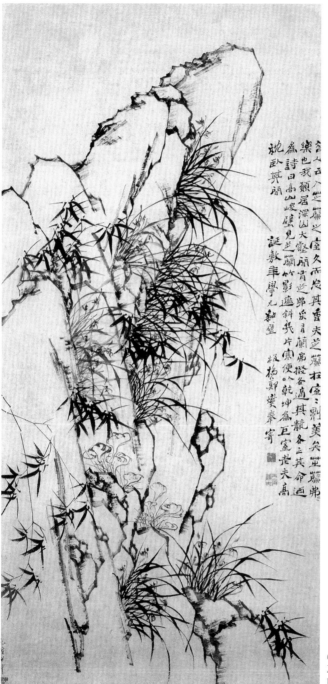

枕臥其間

窈
窕
女
子
人
世
蘭
之
室
久
而
忘
其
香
夫
芝
蘭
柱
室
之
剥
美
矣
世
豈
巖
弟
樂
也
我
顏
居
深
山
大
壑
間
青
延
即
采
青
蘭
常
掇
各
適
其
靜
各
正
其
命
道
爲
詩
曰
高
山
峻
礱
見
芝
蘭
竹
影
遙
斜
戕
片
寒
便
入
乾
坤
爲
巨
室
芷
夫
高

誕
敷
年
學
兄
黏
璧

板
橋
鄭
燮
奉
寄

*Orchid and Bamboo*, by
Zheng Banqiao of the Qing
Dynasty.

were all schools of painters who inherited the literati paintings of the Yuan Dynasty. These painters were all well educated in the classical masterpieces, scripture and history, and had high accomplishment in culture and arts, they, therefore, stressed the self-awareness and the cultivation of personality and morality. They usually gave equal importance to poems, calligraphy and painting in their artistic creations, tried to show their unique artistic personality and were not hindered by the rigid rules. Therefore, during the Ming and Qing dynasties, new artistic charms were added to the traditional themes for the landscape, figure, and flower-bird paintings.

# Furniture

While at home, ancient Chinese used to have the habit of being seated on the floor before they had chairs and stools to sit on. The way their furniture were designed and placed in homes corresponded with the way people got seated.

## Furniture before the Han Dynasty

Before the Han Dynasty, people inhabiting the country's heartland had the habit of being seated on the floor covered with wall-to-wall mats—to be more exact, of kneeling on the floor while squatting on the heels. Sitting with the legs stretched out was resented, seen as disrespectful. Furniture used at the time fell into four categories—those on which people slept or sat including mats, beds and couches, tables long or short on which things were placed, screens and mosquito nets, trunks, toilet cases used by women, and suitcases. All these are low, commensurate to people's habit of being seated on the floor. A couch unearthed from a Han Dynasty tomb is only 19 centimeters tall. Even lower—just five centimeters—is a table from a tomb of the same dynasty at Mawangdui, Changsha, Hunan Province.

## Development of "Furniture with High Legs"

Large numbers of people fled areas north of the Yangtze River to the south during the period of the Wei, Jin and Southern-Northern dynasties when wars were fought incessantly between warlords for control of the country. That chaotic period also saw many

A yellow rosewood armchair of the 17<sup>th</sup> century.

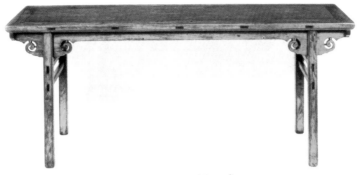

A yellow rosewood long table of the 16<sup>th</sup> century.

nomads migrate from the northwest and northeast to the better-developed heartland. All this compelled the Han Chinese to change their etiquette and customs. While resented by the Han Chinese, for example, sitting with legs stretched out was absolutely normal among immigrants of China's ethnic minority groups. With those nomads there came "furniture with high legs," the likes of chairs and stools.

What we categorize as "furniture with high legs" appear in murals and sculptural artworks done during the Eastern Jin Dynasty and the succeeding period when 16 independent regimes were set up in succession in northern China. Most of these are found in grotto temples, in which the most frequently seen are round stools. Stools of woven plant branches are often seen in murals on Buddhist themes in Korzer Grottoes in Baicheng, Xinjiang, including some wrapped with a kind of textile. Stools are also seen on relieves found in Yungang Grottoes.

Beside round stools, grotto murals at Dunhuang feature square stools. One example is a serial picture telling the story of a Buddhist monk who commits suicide in defying some brutal force that tries to coerce him into acting in violation of Buddha commandments. Two kinds of stools are seen in the picture—those with four legs for each and those drum-like stools without legs. A mural found in Grotto No. 283 depicts a monk sitting cross-legged on an armchair for meditation.

Chairs and stools are also seen in pictures found in secular tombs. One example is a picture cut on the surface of the stone coffin in a tomb of the Northern Qi Dynasty, in which tomb owner is depicted as sitting on a round stool. Folding stools were first used during the Eastern Han Dynasty and had become quite popular by the 16-State Period. From a tomb built in the year 547 archeologists unearthed a clay figurine—obviously a maidservant—with a folding chair in her hand. The tomb owner was identified as belonging to a woman.

As we have mentioned, "furniture with high legs" is found mostly in artworks on Buddhist themes that were produced during the Southern and Northern Dynasties. In comparison, such furniture is more frequently seen in artworks depicting secular life under the Sui and Tang dynasties. This is true especially to murals, as well as to figurines used as funerary objects, indicating that "furniture with high legs" had by then come to be used in people's daily life.

In murals found in the tomb of Prince Li Xian that depicts life in the imperial palace, there are round stools, armchairs and other "furniture pieces with high legs." Another example is the tomb built in the year 756 for General Gao Yuangui of the Tang Dynasty, which has a mural on the south-facing wall that depicts the general sitting on a chair. After archeologists opened one of the tombs belonging to a family named Wei at Nanliwang Village in Anxian County, Shaanxi Province, they found a mural depicting the tomb owner, a woman, sitting on a stool in front of a six-leaf screen. Another mural in the tomb brings back to life a banquet with people sitting on benches round a table. Among pottery and tri-color glazed figurines unearthed from tombs in Xi'an, one is a maidservant sitting on a stool in front of a mirror, and there are also storytellers sitting on benches.

Complete sets of "furniture with high legs" were developed after the Tang Dynasty. Tables, desks, beds and screens are seen in murals in tombs belonging to the period of the Five Dynasties, of which the most representative are those in the tomb belonging to a man named Wang Chuzhi at Quyang County, Hebei Province. "Furture

Yellow rosewood armchairs of the late 16ᵗʰ century.

pieces with high legs" are also seen in ancient paintings. The most famous of such paintings are *Chess Games in Front of a Screen* and *Han Xizai Feasting at Night*, which were done by Zhou Wenju and Gu Hongzhong of the Southern Tang Dynasty (937–975), respectively.

Traditional Chinese furniture, including tables, chairs, screens and clothes stands, became basically finalized in design during the Song and Yuan dynasties, and arrangements of these at homes, relatively fixed. Large quantities of murals and brick carvings have been found in tombs built during the Song and Yuan dynasties, often depicting the husband and wife sitting on high-back chairs, facing each other across a table laden with food, with screens behind them.

Then came the heyday for traditional Chinese furniture, the Ming Dynasty that succeeded the Yuan.

# Ming-style Furniture

To be more exact, traditional Chinese furniture had its heyday from the 15ᵗʰ century to the 17ᵗʰ, a period from the mid-Ming to the early Qing. Many of the furniture pieces produced during this period are exquisite artworks, for which they are broadly referred to as the "Ming-style furniture." Birth of Ming-style furniture can be attributed to an economic boom China was able to enjoy during the period. The rapid development of a commodity economy and the increasing prosperity of cities prompted a keen public interest in furniture. Ocean-going shipping made it possible for rosewood, mahogany, red sandalwood and other quality timber produced in Southeast Asia to become available to the country in sufficient quantities for production of furniture. Moreover, jobs requiring fine workmanship for furniture production became possible thanks to invention of planes and other carpentry tools.

Ming-style furniture pieces fall into five categories, namely, chairs and stools, tables and desks, beds and couches, wardrobes and clothes stands, and miscellaneous pieces.

Meticulous attention to selection of materials is a most salient feature of Ming-style furniture. Pieces that have survived to our time are all produced with quality hard timber. Yellow rosewood was always the first choice. Of the 160 pieces in the *Collection of the Best Ming-Style Furniture* compiled in the 1980s by a group of Chinese mainland and Hong Kong scholars, more than 100 are made of yellow rosewood reputed for its beautiful color and exquisite grain. Ming-style furniture pieces of red sandalwood are favored for a primitive beauty, and those of other hard timbers, for their exquisite veins. Though relatively inexpensive, those of ferrous mesua and beech are equally favored.

A beauty of simplicity in structure makes Ming-style furniture eternally enchanting. This can be attributed to an artistic taste in favor of urbanity and simplicity prevalent not only among the intelligentsia but also among members of the imperial family and nobles—descendants of soldiers who resented things garish and excessively elaborate. Improved carpentry tools were also responsible, with which carpenters were able to do the details to the best of their customers' satisfaction.

Not a single metal nail is used on any piece of Ming-style furniture. In producing a piece of Ming-style furniture, only occasionally does the carpenter use glue to supplement the skill of fixing the mortises and tenons that originated from building of wooden architectural structures.

# Indoor Furnishing

The way furniture pieces are distributed in a house became relatively fixed during the Ming-Qing period. As we can still see, the main hall, sitting room, bedrooms and study in a house typical of the period are invariably fitted with pairs of furniture pieces that are placed in symmetrical order. In a chamber or room, the long table or bed that faces the door and with a window behind is always the center of the furnishing. The room or chamber normally has one long table and two chairs, or four chairs if there are two

A yellow rosewood dressing table of the late 16<sup>th</sup> century.

tables. The wardrobes, bookcases and other furniture pieces are also placed in symmetrical order, sometimes with calligraphic works and antiques placed in between for added taste.

The main decoration in the main hall, or the south-facing hall, is a large painting hung on the wall facing the door. Flanking the painting is a pair of scrolls that form an antithetical couplet. Below the painting there is a long table on which decorative porcelain vessels are placed. A square table for eight people is placed in front of the long table—"eight" being a lucky number that originates from the Taoist legend about the Eight Immortals. At either side of the table there is a large wooden armchair—the so-called "imperial teacher's chair." A square or round table is often placed beside the east or west wall for display of flowers and arts and crafts articles.

The drawing room is, in fact, an extension of the main hall, separated from the main hall by a solid wall or a wall-like screen decorated with carvings, where guests and friends are received. In addition to tables and chairs, it features an exquisitely designed case on which antiques are displayed. The study can either be an extension of the main hall or an independent chamber. Furniture pieces found there include bookshelves, antique cases, a desk, a table and a few chairs.

Heated earthen beds have been popular in north China where it is cold in winter, and people in the south prefer to sleep on wooden beds. In most cases, a wooden bed is fitted with a frame for a mosquito net. An elaborately decorated bed, however, may look like a small chamber in itself. Ancient Chinese men like to wear long hair, hence those dressing table found in virtually all bedrooms. The habit may be attributed to this Confucian motto on filial duties: "No damage must be done to your body and hair because they are given to you by your parents." Elaborating, we may safely say that Ming-style furniture was a part of the culture characteristic of China's patriarchal society of feudalism. It resulted from an economic prosperity the country was able to enjoy in the late period of China's feudal society, and ceased to develop as feudalism kept declining.

# Arts and Crafts

# Gold and Silver Artifacts

A gilded silver perfume holder of the Tang Dynasty.

The story goes back to one night in 1987 when a tower in an ancient temple in Xi'an, Shaanxi Province, collapsed in wind and rain. The Famen Temple was built during the Tang Dynasty. When clearing the debris, workers found an underground palace closed in the year 874, which turned out to be a stunning treasure house. From the front, middle and rear chambers of the palace about 400 relics were unearthed, which were to be identified as artifacts used by several Tang emperors for Buddha worshipping. Of these, 121 are gold and silver artifacts whose beauty and extravagance are beyond people's imagination. There is a set of eight gold and silver cases, one smaller than the other and one inside the other, which was produced on order of Emperor Yi Zong. The innermost case is of pure gold, in which people found Sarira, or a Buddha bone. Discovery of the underground palace aroused global attention, in part due to those gold and silver artifacts unearthed from there.

Production of gold and silver articles in China dates back to the Shang-Zhou period, but so far archeologists have been able to find only a limited number of earrings and other small personal ornaments produced at the time. Relatively large gold and silver articles did not appear until the Warring States Period. One example is a gold cup with a lid, along with a gold spoon in it, which was unearthed from the tomb of a duke in Suixian County, Hubei Province. We have to note that gold and silver articles produced before the Han Dynasty are exceptionally rare. Gold was circulated as an instrument of payment. Nevertheless, we do find bronze vessels with gold decorations or with their surface gilded or inlaid with patterns of gold thread. This state of affairs did not change much even during the Han Dynasty.

Gold and silver objects became increasingly popular among China's aristocrats as time went by, beginning the period of the Southern and Northern Dynasties. Most gold and silver articles used at the time were imported from Persia and other foreign lands, the likes of bottles, plates and bowls in strange shapes, as well as necklaces and finger rings. Gold and silver cups and gold necklaces unearthed from a Sui Dynasty tomb built in 608 may have been produced in what is now Pakistan or Afghanistan. Also unearthed from the tomb of Li Jingxun, granddaughter of the eldest daughter of Emperor Wen Di of the Sui Dynasty, is a gold bracelet inlaid with blue and green glass beads, which might have been imported from India. Li Jingxun died when she was only nine years old. The sheer number of gold and silver objects in her tomb testifies to how popular such objects were among members of the upper class.

Mass production of gold and silver objects began during the

Picture shows a pot and a table spoon, both of gold, produced during the Warring States Period, which were unearthed from the tomb of a duke at Suixian, Hubei Province.

**The Sasanian Empire**
The Sasanian Empire was the last dynasty of the ancient Persian Empire, and its ruling lasted from 226 to 651. After the founding of the Sasanian Empire, it continuously fought wars with the Roman Empire and Byzantine Empire. Its territory often changed, and during its prime time, its boundary extended to the Euphrates River in the west, to the Persian Gulf in the south, to Caucasus, Armenia and Amu Darya in central Asia in the north, and to Pamir in the east. The Sasanian Empire had frequent exchanges with ancient China. After the empire was overthrown, its prince Pirooz escaped to China and became an official in the Tang Dynasty.

period of the Sui and early-Tang Dynasty. More often than not, gold and silver objects produced at the time are imitations of those from Central Asia or what is broadly referred to as the West Region while assuming some Chinese characteristics. One example is a gilded octagonal silver cup unearthed from a tomb at Hejia Village, Shaanxi Province, which is Sasanian in shape with relieves presenting Chinese musicians and dancers. There are also silver cups in Sasanian style but decorated with traditional Chinese hunting patterns.

Gold and silver objects had their heyday during the Sui and Tang dynasties due to an unprecedented economic boom and increased communication between China and the rest of the world via the Silk Road. The imperial family of the Tang Dynasty, in particular, created a huge demand for things of gold and silver. Poet Wang Jian of the Tang wrote of a palace feast: "Five thousand gold plates are used, laden with bright red peony flowers of butter." The poem may be an artistic exaggeration, but may testify to the fact that huge quantities of gold and silver eating utensils were used in the imperial palace. Chang'an, the national capital, was center of production, where there was a handicraft workshop producing to meet imperial needs. The workshop was expanded during the reign of Emperor Xuan Zong (847–859) as imperial needs grew. During the late period of the dynasty, production of gold and silver articles spread to areas on the lower and middle reaches of the Yangtze River in the south and, in artistic style and quality, products produced there were as good as those produced in the national capital. An elaborate range of techniques was employed in production, including sheet-metal working, casting, welding, cutting, polishing, hammering and carving. More often than not, several techniques were used in producing just one piece.

As time went by, gold and silver objects became "purely" Chinese in design and artistic style. Painstaking attention to artistic design characterizes gold and silver objects of the Tang Dynasty—to be more precise, of the shapes of plates, cups, boxes and pots. Those large plates with floral patterns of gold are the most striking examples, which take the shape of water chestnut flower or sunflower formed with fine, delicate lines. A sander burner is probably the most ingeniously constructed. The ball consists of two half-spheres with holes cut in beautiful patterns to allow emission of smoke. The half-spheres each are fitted with a device of concentric circle to ensure balance of the sander holder. Artifacts noted for exquisite craftsmanship also include a gilded silver pot with rings in the shape of a horse and a gilded wine cup with a base in the shape of a turtle.

Gold and silver artifacts of the Tang Dynasty are also reputed for those decorative patterns on them. Many silver vessels have

Picture shows a gilded silver basket unearthed from an underground chamber in Famen Temple built during the Tang Dynasty.

Photo shows a gold pagoda in Tibetan style, which was left over from the Qing Dynasty.

gilded patterns. Especially worth mentioning are those large plates in shapes of chestnut flower or sunflower, which have in the center deer, lion or fish-like dragon patterns. In many cases, circular floral patterns are done round the main pattern in the center of a plate.

Gold and silver artifacts were popular not only among monarchs and aristocrats of the Tang Dynasty but also among the land gentry and other rich people. From a single Tang tomb at Hejia Village in Xi'an archeologists unearthed a large quantity of gold and silver artifacts, testifying to the widespread use of such artifacts at the time. Gold and silver objects continued to be popular in dynasties following the Tang. Among tombs from which large quantities of gold and silver artifacts have been unearthed, the most famous is the tomb of Emperor Shen Zong and his queen, one of the 13 imperial tombs of the Ming Dynasty in Beijing. Though commoners of the Ming Dynasty, Dong Si, Wan Gui and Wan Tong, also in Beijing, had many funerary objects of gold and silver in their tombs.

# Lacquer Works

Lacquer works constitute a special branch of China's traditional arts and crafts, which are objects with wooden or silk skeletons smooth or glossy with the inner and outer surfaces coated with several to a few dozen layers of lacquer. Lacquer coating was done just for decoration when people were yet to know that lacquer is resistant to acid and alkali erosion and is also humidity-proof. The oldest lacquer ware, in fact a wooden bowl, was unearthed from ruins of the Hemudu Culture at Yuyao County, Zhejiang Province, which was produced about 7,000 years ago. Bits of a

**The Hemudu Culture**
The Hemudu Culture is an ancient Neolithic culture in the lower reaches of the Yangtze River in China, and it was so named after it was first discovered at Hemudu in Yuyao, Zhejiang province. The culture is mainly distributed in the Ningshao plain on the southern bank of the Hangzhou Bay and the Zhoushan Island, and dates back to 5,000–3,300 BC. During the Hemudu Culture, agriculture highlighted by rice growing was its economic activities, and people then also engaged in animal husbandry, fisheries and hunting. The dwelling places of the people then formed villages of different sizes.

red paint on the bowl's inside are seen, which has been identified as a kind of raw lacquer. From ruins of the Liangzhu Culture that existed 3,000 years ago in the same province, archeologists found a lacquered cup inlaid with jade pieces, suggesting that people living at the time were already acquainted with combined use of lacquering and jade carving to produce artworks. In other words, lacquer works of the Liangzhu Culture were no longer purely for practical use.

Lacquer works produced from the 21$^{st}$ century BC to the fifth century BC have been unearthed in many parts of China, including Beijing, Henan, Hebei, Shandong, Shaanxi, Gansu and Anhui. These serve as material evidence to the initial period of boom for development of lacquer working, a period spanning the Xian, Shang and Zhou dynasties. Lacquer working peaked during the Warring States Period, coinciding with a decline of bronze ware production. It is against this background that lacquer works, light in weight and more decorative, found their way into the life of the upper class. Numerous lacquer works produced during that period have been unearthed, and those unearthed from tombs of the Chu Kingdom are in the largest number and also are the most exquisite in workmanship.

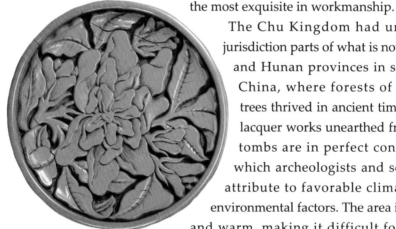

The Chu Kingdom had under its jurisdiction parts of what is now Hubei and Hunan provinces in southern China, where forests of lacquer trees thrived in ancient times. Most lacquer works unearthed from Chu tombs are in perfect conditions, which archeologists and scientists attribute to favorable climatic and environmental factors. The area is humid and warm, making it difficult for cracks to form in the course of lacquer coating. Moreover, water in the area is chemically

A plate produced by Zhang Cheng, a master handicraftsman of the Yuan Dynasty.

neutral, without much acid or alkali. Lacquer works identified as belonging to the Chu King include not only small things like cups, wine sets and boxes, but also much larger things, such as coffins, beds, hangers for musical chimes and bells. There are even weapons with lacquered surfaces. Red and black are the basic colors of lacquer works produced in the Chu Kingdom. People living at the time seemed to know that red and black lacquers, while forming a beautiful color contrast, are most chemically stable. Small things like cups mostly have the outside coated with black lacquer and the inside, with red lacquer. Lacquer paintings invariably have a black-and-red background, with the lines done with lacquers diverse in color—red, yellow, blue, white, as well as deep blue, green, brown, golden and silvery.

For centuries after the Han Dynasty collapsed, lacquer works seemed to be elbowed out of people's life by an increasing use of porcelain ware. Few lacquer works unearthed so far were products of the period from the end of the Han to the Song and Yuan dynasties. But lacquer works produced during a period from the Three Kingdoms to the Tang Dynasty are no inferior

A cosmetics box produced by Zhang Cheng, a master handicraftsman of the Yuan Dynasty.

in workmanship to products produced earlier. In 1984, Some 80 lacquer paintings were unearthed from a tomb of the East Wu Kingdom at Ma'anshan, Anhui Province. These stunned the archeological world for superb workmanship and artistic value, which serve as important material evidence to study of traditional Chinese fine art.

Production of lacquer works peaked again during the Yuan, Ming and Qing dynasties. This period saw lacquer works change into pure artworks and their production techniques attain the highest level of perfection, with a variety of new techniques developed including what is known to experts as "lacquer carving."

"Lacquer carving" involves an elaborate process of doing human figures and pictures on lacquer coating comprising several dozen to well over 100 layers, which have a combined thickness of more than ten millimeters. During the Yuan Dynasty, Zhejiang and Jiangsu provinces had the best lacquer work artists in the country, among whom the most prominent were Zhang Cheng and Yang

A hand warmer with lacquer painting. It was produced in the 16th century.

Mao in Jiaxing, Zhejiang. The Palace Museum has in its collection a lacquered plate with a jasmine flower design, the inscriptions on it reading "made by Zhang Cheng." A lacquered vase made by Yang Mao, which has carved designs on it, is also found in the collection.

Many lacquer works production centers were developed during the Ming Dynasty, including Zhejiang, Yunnan for carved lacquer works, Yangzhou for lacquer works inlaid with decorative pieces, Suzhou for gilded lacquer works, and Shanxi for gilded lacquered furniture. What merits special mention is Huang Dacheng, a master lacquer works artist in Xin'an, Anhui Province, who lived during the reign of Emperor QianLong of the Qing Dynasty. Basing himself on past experiences and experiences of his own, he authored ancient China's only monograph on lacquer works production. The book has 14 chapters, separately on production techniques, raw materials, tools and lacquer coating.

Among lacquer works produced in the 18th century, during the successive reigns of emperors Yong Zheng and Qian Long of the Qing Dynasty, the best were still from Zhejiang, Jiangsu and other parts of southern China. Guangdong and Fujian provinces were the greatest exporters of lacquer works. On order of Emperor Qian Long, experts in ivory carving were involved in production of lacquer works exclusively for imperial use. Despite that, Suzhou in Jiangsu Province remained the most important center for lacquer works production not only for the general public but also on imperial orders. We need to note that the emperor was reputed for a high aesthetic taste. Thanks to that, arts and crafts production enjoyed an unprecedented boom during his reign. Problem is that some of the products are too elaborately decorated though still of a high artistic value. Lacquer works produced in Yangzhou, also in Jiangsu, furnish a case in point. These are often inlaid with pieces of a dozen expensive materials including for example gold, silver, precious stones, pearls, jadeite, agate and hawksbill turtle shell, forming pictures of landscapes, human figures, birds, flowers and architectural structures.

# Bamboo, Wooden, Ivory and Animal Horn Articles

Among bamboo carvings produced in ancient China, the earliest are those excavated from a tomb of the Western Han Dynasty. Fragmented bamboo carvings have been found in tombs belonging to the Western Xia Dynasty that once ruled parts of northern China. Bamboo carvings are documented in classic literature produced after the Southern and Northern Dynasties, but little material evidence has been found as bamboo gets rotten easily.

During the mid-Ming Dynasty, bamboo carving became an independent branch of the traditional Chinese art. The most

An ivory cup of the Shang Dynasty.

eminent bamboo artists were Zhu He, his son Zhu Ying and his grandson Zhu Zhuzhi, who lived in the late Ming period in Jiading, or what is now Shanghai. They were credited with the Jiading school of bamboo carving that was to influence development of the art in the following centuries. While inheriting what is the best in the school, Wu Zhipan of the early Qing Dynasty developed the art by using bamboo carving techniques to do wooden carvings. Wu's works are reputed for exquisite workmanship and a three-dimension effect. Of these, the most representative is a boxwood writing brush holder in the collection of the Palace Museum, which has on its surface a carved picture depicting announcement of victory in a war. It stuns the viewer with numerous figures and landscape done in relief in so limited a space.

Many scholars of the Ming Dynasty and the succeeding Qing took bamboo carving as a pastime, partly because bamboo was inexpensive and easy to carve on relative to gold, jade, bronze and stone. Despite that, hardly was any large-sized bamboo and bamboo root carving were produced, due to limitations of the material. What have survived to our time are mostly small things for practical use, the likes of writing brush, incense holders and ink and seal boxes.

By "wood carvings," we mean those small wooden antiques, with carvings of human figures and/or landscapes on them, not those huge wooden statues in ancient temples. As a traditional art form, wood carvings, mostly on Confucian, Taoist and Buddhist themes, experienced a rapid development in the Ming and Qing dynasties. Ming-style beds popular in southern China often have on them relieves based on stories about filial children and immortals, as well as stories told in the classic Chinese novel *Romance of the Three Kingdoms* and in traditional opera pieces. Also produced in the Ming and Qing dynasties are small decorations with carvings, including for example *ru yi*, bars with auspicious patterns carved in relief.

Balls within balls, incense holders and fans and mats of ivory splints are the most representative of ivory articles produced during the Ming-Qing period. Rhino horns, with medicinal contents that dissolve in

Bamboo root carving depicting "Li with an iron crutch," one of the eight Taoist immortals. It was produced during the Qing Dynasty.

alcohol, were often carved into wine cups. Such cups could also be objects for artistic appreciation for their color and luster and the workmanship for their production. Ox horns were often used as substitutes for rhino horns that had to be imported and therefore were expensive.

# Artificially Shaped Gourds

An artificially shaped gourd is produced by having the growth of a gourd still small and tender on veins conditioned in a mould, so that when ripe, the gourd will have the same shape as the mould along with the decorative pattern carved on the inner wall of the mould. The best artificially shaped gourds were produced when China was under emperors Kang Xi and Qian Long of the Qing Dynasty, mostly taking the shapes of bottles, bowls, basins and boxes. The rate of success was very low for production of artificially shaped gourds. It often occurred that out of several hundred young gourds in moulds, only one or two could be rated as artistically satisfactory after the moulds were removed. For this reason, many artificially shaped gourds that have survived to our time are priceless antiques. These fall into two categories—those purely for decoration and those in which singing insects are raised during winter.

A bottle, in fact an artificially shaped gourd, produced during the reign of Emperor Yong Zheng of the Qing Dynasty.

# Embroidery

Embroidery of the Ming-Qing period is diverse in artistic style, and is done on a range of materials including brocade, satin, silk cloth, silk gauze and crape. Brocade, which originated from the Song and Yuan Dynasty, became the most popular silk textile in the country during the Ming Dynasty. A range of varieties was developed with techniques combining jacquard weaving and gold thread weaving, including brocade with blind flower designs, shot brocade, tapestry satin and tapestry satin with flower designs.

Far back in the Song Dynasty, products of embroidery and cut silk brocade had already become divided into two main categories, those for practical use and those for artistic appreciation. Pursuit of the same artistic effect as traditional Chinese paintings characterizes embroidery and cut silk brocade of the Ming-Qing period. A most striking example is the Gu school of embroidery, which has remained famous to this day for products dubbed as "embroidered paintings." The most representative "embroidered paintings," so to speak, are attributed to a woman named Han, which were produced by copying famous paintings of the Song-Yuan period. Embroidered paintings and calligraphic works, many on Buddhist themes, were done on cut silk brocade, too.

Chinese embroidery, particularly folk embroidery not produced for commercial purpose, has always been favored by collectors across the world. China is the birthplace of silk and silk textiles. In ancient China, families followed the maxim "men doing the crops while women engaging in weaving and spinning," which was not only the prevalent way of living but also the philosophical and ethical basis for the Chinese society. For well over 2,000 years, needlework was compulsory for women. In following the tradition, betrothed girls would be busy working on anything and everything that could be judged by families of their future husbands as material evidence to their virtue, ranging from screens, sheets and towels to their own underwear. This may be a major cultural factor that contributed to development of embroidery in ancient China.

# Cloisonne

The Chinese for cloisonne is *jing tai lan*, "*jing tai*" being the name of a Ming Dynasty emperor during whose reign mass production of such articles began and lan, meaning "blue" — in most cases the background color of *jing tai lan*. Cloisonne enamel techniques were brought from Persia into China's Yunnan Province during the Yuan Dynasty. These were improved during the Ming Dynasty by incorporating them with some of the traditional techniques for metal inlaying and porcelain making, which eventually gave birth to a new kind of cloisonne called *jing tai lan*. To produce a jing tai lan or Chinese cloisonne vase, for example, the workman needs to produce a copper roughcast, welds some decorative patterns of copper wires to the roughcast, inlays the empty space with enamel and, last of all, fires the "decorated" roughcast in a kiln. If all goes well, the finished product will be elegant with a crystal or deep blue background and dazzling with red, green, yellow and white enamel that throws the golden yellow decorative patterns

Cloisonne enamel tea things.

in sharp relief. *Jing tai lan* articles could be large—for example, a Tibetan-style pagoda in the Palace Museum collection is 2.3 meters tall. There are also small things like jewel cases and toothpick holders, which are available in souvenir shops across the country. *Jing tai lan* articles have been popular all the time, and are still in mass production. Generally speaking, those produced during the Ming Dynasty have relatively heavy roughcasts, and are relatively simple in design. Those produced during the early Qing period, however, seem to be a bit too polished due to an over stress on their elegance. In comparison, those of the late Qing period are markedly crude in workmanship and superfluous in style.

# Purple Clay Teapots

Purple clay teapots are a special kind of pottery, which are distinguished mainly by their shapes, not by those decorative patterns on them. Yixiang City, Jiangsu Province, is the best-known producer of such teapots, where porcelain clay, in diverse colors including purple, purplish red and green, is exceptionally fine and highly plastic. Purple clay teapots retain the flavor of tea and, the longer they are used, the brighter will their surface be. They are artworks while good for practical use.

After the mid-Ming Dynasty, many scholars in southern China, in a bid to exhibit their artistic taste, became keen to purple clay teapots. Thanks to their participation in production, teapots in exotic shapes, in shapes of wax gourds, lotus flowers, bamboo joints, drums, goose eggs, etc., came into being. Some that have survived to our time do bear carved pictures and inscriptions for added beauty. Nevertheless, purple clay teapots without carved decorations are most preferred.

It is not difficult to assess the quality of a purple clay teapot. You may lift up the teapot and see whether the handle, lid and spouts are on a straight line. Then you feel its surface to see if it is fine and smooth. Then you remove the lid and examine how well

A Ming Dynasty purple clay teapot.

the inner part of the teapot is connected with its spout. Last of all, you place the teapot upside down on a table and examine whether the handle, lid and spout are exactly on the same plane. Though the body of the teapot and its lid were fired simultaneously in the same kiln, contraction of the two parts may vary, on which the quality of the teapot counts. By following the process given above, you'll distinguish a genuine antique from a fake one and one of good quality from one of inferior quality. For purple clay teapots, quality is of paramount importance, not necessarily the date of their production carved on them. "The older a thing is, the higher will be its price"—this conventional way of assessing the value of antiques does not always apply to purple clay teapots.

# The Collection and Preservation
# of Cultural Relics

# Collecting in the Flourishing Age

As a folk saying goes, "buying gold in the troubled times, and collecting in the flourishing age."

In the ancient history of China, all flourishing dynasties were also the golden eras for collection and appreciation of cultural relics. The Shang Dynasty was the first dynasty in China which had detailed historical records and rich cultural heritage. Cultural relics show that the rulers then collected an astonishing amount of jade, gems and treasure. For example, in the tomb of Fu Hao, the wife of a Shang Dynasty king named Wu Ding, more than 1,600 pieces of various treasures were buried, including 755 pieces of jade wares. The last king of the Shang Dynasty, Zhou, constructed the Lutai palaces to store the precious treasures paid to the Shang as tributes by the subordinate kingdoms. Later, when King Wu of the Zhou Dynasty attacked and stormed into the Shang capital, King Zhou, who had no way to escape, ran to the Lutai palaces, put numerous pearls, jade and treasures on his body and burnt himself death.

The imperial court families of the Han Dynasty paid special emphasis to the collection of cultural relics. Emperor Wudi of the Han Dynasty set up a secret hall to store valuable books and famous paintings, and also to store bronze wares made during the reign of Huangong of the Qi Kingdom during the Warring States Period. According to the *Chronicles of the Han Dynasty—Records of Suburban Sacrifices*, Emperor Xuandi of the Han Dynasty also set up a special hall in the Weiyang Palace to store and keep valuable jade and precious ancient bronze vessels. Emperor Mingdi Liu Zhuang of the Eastern Han Dynasty (reigned 58–75) "had special favor in paintings and opened his painting studio," and collected numerous valuable paintings.

During the prime time of the Tang Dynasty that lasted for more than 200 years, all, from emperors down to the officials, were zealous of collecting cultural relics. It is said Emperor Taizong, Li Shimin, instructed others to cheat and obtain the authentic copy of *Preface to the Orchid Pavilion Collection* by master calligrapher Wang Xizhi (303–361) of the Jin Dynasty, and buried it with him in his tomb at the Zhao Tombs of the Tang Dynasty. The family of Zhang Yanyuan in the Tang Dynasty, author of the *Records of Historical Famous Paintings*, produced three prime ministers and had five generations who served as senior officials in the imperial court. This family, in the lasting peace and prosperity of the Tang Dynasty, collected numerous paintings by famous painters by taking advantage of their special political status. In the *Records of Historical Famous Paintings*, Zhang Yanyuan wrote: "Any real collector must have famous scroll paintings by Gu, Lu, Zhang and Wu, and only then he could say he has a collection of paintings..." By saying so, he meant, if you claimed to be a painting connoisseur, you should at least have famous scroll paintings by Gu Kaizhi, Lu Tanwei, Zhang Sengyao and Wu Daozi. From this, we could come to know how popular art collection was and what best works they collected in the Tang Dynasty.

In the Song dynasties, the studies of the bronze and stone inscriptions emerged, and many scholars joined in the studies. The preconditions for such studies were the collections of bronze wares and stone inscriptions, and researches into them. Emperor Huizong of the Song Dynasty ordered to compile the *Xuanhe Collection of Archaeological Artifacts* to record and detail more than 800 pieces of bronze wares kept by the imperial family in the Xuanhe Palace, and all of them were big bronze wares from the Xia, Shang and Zhou dynasties. Each piece of the bronze would be accompanied with an illustration drawing, its size, weight, rubbing of its inscriptions and explanations, and some of them would also have their unearthed places and the names of the former collectors. At the same time, Emperor Huizong also ordered to compile the *Xuanhe Register of Paintings* and the *Xuanhe Register of Books*, with the first recording and detailing more than 6,300 pieces of paintings by more than 230 painters after the Wei and Jin dynasties, and the latter recording and detailing more than 1,300 works by about 200 calligraphers.

Renowned scholar Ouyang Xiu (1007–1072) of the Song Dynasty collected some 1,000 volumes of rubbings of stone inscriptions and mounted them into books.

In the Qing Dynasty, the scale of cultural relics collection was further expanded, and research into cultural relics was further deepened. In particular, Emperor Kangxi, Emperor Yongzheng and Emperor Qianlong were all well-versed in traditional Chinese culture and were all very fond of ancient arts. They, as emperors, led the trend in the collection, appreciation and research of cultural relics, and helped cultivate a big number of renowned connoisseurs and researchers in cultural relics. According to the catalogues of the imperial court of the Qing Dynasty, the collections by famous connoisseurs of the Qing Dynasty as Liang Qingbiao (1620–1691) Sun Chengze (1592–1676), Geng Zhaozhong (1640–1686) and Bian Yongyu (1645–1712) were all included in the treasure collections by the imperial court. This was considered the biggest convergence of top cultural relics in China since the Song Dynasty.

# Treasures Lost in the Troubled Times

If the losses of cultural relics in wars and natural disasters in several thousand years of Chinese history were not calculated, the most recent massive losses of Chinese cultural relics occurred in the late years of the Qing Dynasty and the early years of the Republic of China. Of these massive losses, the most disastrous losses are the following:

**The burning of the Old Summer Palace** The Old Summer Palace, located in northwestern Beijing, used to be a masterpiece of Chinese architecture and gardens. This served as one of the residences and offices of the emperors in the late Qing Dynasty, was composed of towers, pavilions and palaces of both the Chinese and Western architectural styles, and was a place where various cultural relics and artistic works were stored and displayed. During the Second Opium War in 1860, the Anglo-French Allied Forces attacked and stormed into the Old Summer Palace, started a crazy looting and then torched and burned it down. The secretary of the Anglo army recorded the then crazy looting and burning scenes:

"On October 17, the command of the allied forces gave the order to loot. Then, the Anglo and French officers and solders began to loot crazily, and each of them looted a lot of treasures… The French army was stationed in front the garden. The French soldiers, with wooden sticks in hands, looted all treasures that could be carried away, and if they encountered treasures that could not be carried away as bronze wares, porcelain and valuable Nanmu, they smashed them with sticks…."

In recent years, some cultural relics looted from the Old Summer Palace frequently appeared on international auction market, and the most important treasures were the bronze heads of the 12 animals used to symbolize the year of birth originally erected in front of the Haiyan Hall beside the fountain. Of these bronze heads, that of the ox, tiger, monkey, hog, horse, mouse and rabbit had already appeared, with some being purchased back, the whereabouts of the snake, goat, rooster and dog heads still remained unknown.

**The losses of cultural relics on the ancient Silk Road in northwest China** From the 19<sup>th</sup> century to the early years of the 20<sup>th</sup> century, some explorers and scholars from the Western countries entered into China for exploration and research. And along with their exploration and research activities, looting and damages occurred, and numerous Chinese cultural relics were therefore lost and shipped to foreign countries. Of these valuable cultural relics, the most important ones were the ancient documents, written scriptures and Buddhist paintings unearthed from the scripture cave at the Mogao Grottoes in Dunhuang on the ancient Silk Road in northwest China.

From 1900 to 1913, Hungarian Marc Aurel Stein (1862–1943), hired by Britain, went into the northwestern region of China three times, dug and robbed several ancient sites and ancient tombs in Xinjiang and robbed a big quantity of wooden slips with inscriptions, documents and ancient artworks. In particular, from the scripture cave discovered not long ago at the Mogao Grottoes in Dunhuang, he chose and robbed a big quantity of scripture books and Buddhist paintings, packed them in more than 20 wooden boxes and shipped them back to London. Later, Frenchman Paul Pelliot (1878–1945) traced his steps and also came. He was well-versed in Chinese, had a good understanding of the traditional Chinese culture, and made better choice of cultural relics to loot than Stein who did not know Chinese language. From the scripture cave of the Mogao Grottoes, he robbed and took away the best cultural relics, and of them, the written volumes were kept in the Oriental section of the National Library of France, and the silk paintings and silk products were kept in the Guimet Museum.

In addition, there were many more foreigners who went to the northwestern region of China to rob and loot cultural relics during that time, including Swedish Sven Andera Hedin (1865–1952), Russian Sergei Oldenburg (1863–1934), and Japanese Otani Kozui (1876–1948) and Tachibana Zuicho (1890–1968), and they raided and robbed many treasures and artworks which are still kept in the museums in their countries.

**Insider theft during the reign of the last emperor**  If we say that the raids and lootings of Chinese cultural relics by Westerners were bandit activities, the losses of cultural relics from the imperial court of the Qing Dynasty, orchestrated by Puyi, the last emperor of the Qing Dynasty, could be regarded as insider theft. As early as in 1924, three years before Puyi was ordered to evacuate the imperial palace, he, in the name of "largess" or "borrowing," transferred a big volume of precious books from the Song and Yuan dynasties, and books and paintings from the Jin, Tang and Song dynasties out of the palace, and then packed in more than 70 wooden boxes and secretly transported to the British concession in Tianjin for storage. In his autobiography *From Emperor to Citizen*, Puyi admits:

"The paintings and ancient books transferred out of the palaces are all treasures, the best of the bests. At that time, the officials and masters of the Imperial Household Department were sorting and counting those paintings and books, so I chose among the best they have selected." "The total number of paintings and books transferred out of the palace was more than 1,000, more than 200 kinds of hanging scrolls and copies, and about 200 kinds of books from the Song Dynasty... They were transported to Tianjin, and dozens of them were sold later. After the founding of Manchukou, Yasunao Yoshioka, an officer of the Japan Kwantung Army, transported these treasures to the northeast, and after the surrender of the Japanese army, the whereabouts of these treasures became unknown."

With the above mentioned batches of cultural relics included, precious cultural relics robbed by and lost in foreign countries in about a century were numerous, most of them are now kept in foreign museums, some are also the collections of private connoisseurs (these cultural relics are often unknown to the public). The most important and well-known cultural relics in foreign museums include:

A bronze wine vessel of the Shang Dynasty, collected by the Freer Gallery of Art, USA.

The Metropolitan Museum of Art in New York is the largest art museum in the United States, has a rich collection of Chinese cultural relics as bronze wares from the Shang and Zhou dynasties, and various stone sculptures, wood sculptures, paintings and porcelains ranging from the Southern and Northern Dynasty to the Yuan Dynasty. And the most famous relic is the relief *Emperor as Donor with Attendants* from the relief sculpture showing the emperor and empress offering to the Buddha in the Longmen Grottoes in Luoyang (the *Empress as Donor with Attendants* is now in the Nelson-Atkins Museum of Art). The University of Pennsylvania Museum of Archaeology and Anthropology, located in Philadelphia, now keeps two horse sculptures from the Zhaoling Mausoleum, the tomb of Emperor Taizong Li Shimin of the Tang Dynasty. There were six horse sculptures at the tomb.

The British Museum in Britain has the biggest collection of Chinese cultural relics in Europe. The most valuable of cultural

relics kept by this museum is the painting *Admonitions of the Instructress to the Palace Ladies* by Gu Kaizhi of the Jin Dynasty. In addition, this museum also keeps the sitting wooden statue of Avalokitesvara, the standing statue of Lokapala from the Tang Dynasty, the painted flag, silk painting, written scriptures and documents from the Tang Dynasty from the scripture cave in Dunhuang, and all of them are priceless

Silk painting of *The Amitabha*, unearthed from Dunhuang Mogao Caves, collected by the British Museum.

*Saluzi*, one of the six stone horses sculpted in Zhao Mausoleum, the mausoleum of Emperor Taizong of Tang Dynasty, collected by Museum of the University of Pennsylvania, U.S.A.

treasures in the world.

France is a center of collections of Chinese cultural relics, next only to Britain. The Louvre Museum in Paris is the center of the collections of Chinese cultural relics in France. The Guimet Museum, a branch of the Louvre Museum, has a special museum of Asian cultural relics, and more than half of its collections are Chinese cultural relics, totaling more than 30,000 pieces, including more than 6,000 pieces of porcelains and a big quantity of painted pottery, bronze, painting scrolls from Dunhuang and paintings from the Song, Yuan and Ming dynasties.

Japan, from the Meiji Reform, began to collect Chinese cultural relics in a well-planned manner, and museums, galleries, temples, consortia and some private connoisseurs across Japan have a collection of Chinese cultural relics totaling hundreds of thousands pieces. In Japan, cultural relics are classified into categories as national treasure, important cultural treasure and cultural treasure, and more than 100 pieces of Chinese cultural relics in Japan are classified as national treasures and tens of thousands pieces are classified as important cultural treasure. Many Japanese museums and art galleries have their special halls for storage and display of Chinese cultural relics. Of them, the Tokyo National Museum boosts the richest collections of Chinese cultural relics, and has five special halls to display Chinese cultural relics.

# Arduous Task ahead for the Protection of Cultural Relics

In more than half a century since 1949, the Chinese government has made painstaking efforts in fighting for the return of Chinese cultural relics lost overseas and in protecting the cultural relics, and has resorted to various channels to win the return of precious cultural relics, Due to the special non-reconstructable property of cultural relics and the desire for huge profits, however, Chinese relics are still in the danger of being lost.

At present, the growing activities of cultural relic smuggling worldwide lead to the grave situation that ancient artworks and cultural relics are landed in the hands of public and private connoisseurs of the developed countries. Take Chinese cultural relics as an example. After the auction activities of Chinese traditional paintings and books in the Western countries were suspended due to the difficulty in determining their authenticity, ancient stone sculptures and clay figure works became a new market favor, in particular, the prices of stone sculptures and clay figures directly unearthed from ancient ruins, ancient tombs and ancient temple have rocketed. In recent years, frequent robbery and theft cases of stone sculptures and clay figures from the ancient tombs, kiln sites, grottoes and temples in China occurred, and such cases usually happened under this background and were related to the rocketing prices of these artworks.

In fact, as early as in 1970, the United Nations adopted the *United Nations Convention Against Illicit Traffic*, which gives special emphasis on the concept that cultural property may not be separated from the places of their origin. For one ancient artwork, it would have and show its connotation completely and accurately only when it is kept in the environment it originally belonged to. This concept spurred the museums and connoisseurs in the developed countries to reflect their roles, and also directly promoted the International Council of Museums to adopt the code of conducts in regulating their activities in acquiring and transferring artworks. At the same time, the pressure on the suppliers of the international art market is also growing for them to be accountable for the sources of their goods. The international conventions now being improved also challenge the past practices, and urge and force the merchants of artworks to be cautious.

In recent years, the Chinese government has increased its support for the protection of cultural relics. On the one hand, it has enacted and modified relevant laws and regulations, cracked down on the robbery, theft and smuggling of cultural relics, and on the other hand, it also strengthened cooperation with relevant countries. In a word, China has made remarkable achievements in the protection of cultural relics, and still, it has a long and arduous task ahead to accomplish.

# Appendix:
## Chronological Table of the Chinese Dynasties

| | |
|---|---|
| The Paleolithic Period | Approx. 1,700,000–10,000 years ago |
| The Neolithic Age | Approx. 10,000–4,000 years ago |
| Xia Dynasty | 2070–1600 BC |
| Shang Dynasty | 1600–1046 BC |
| Western Zhou Dynasty | 1046–771 BC |
| Spring and Autumn Period | 770–476 BC |
| Warring States Period | 475–221 BC |
| Qin Dynasty | 221–206 BC |
| Western Han Dynasty | 206 BC–AD 25 |
| Eastern Han Dynasty | 25–220 |
| Three Kingdoms | 220–280 |
| Western Jin Dynasty | 265–317 |
| Eastern Jin Dynasty | 317–420 |
| Northern and Southern Dynasties | 420–589 |
| Sui Dynasty | 581–618 |
| Tang Dynasty | 618–907 |
| Five Dynasties | 907–960 |
| Northern Song Dynasty | 960–1127 |
| Southern Song Dynasty | 1127–1279 |
| Yuan Dynasty | 1206–1368 |
| Ming Dynasty | 1368–1644 |
| Qing Dynasty | 1616–1911 |
| Republic of China | 1912–1949 |
| People's Republic of China | Founded in 1949 |